[illegible]

with all my love.

To my mother

and in memory of my father,

32 years a railwayman.

Eveline – love from, Hugh

RAILS TO CORWEN

(A story of the building of the railway in the Vale of Edeyrnion)

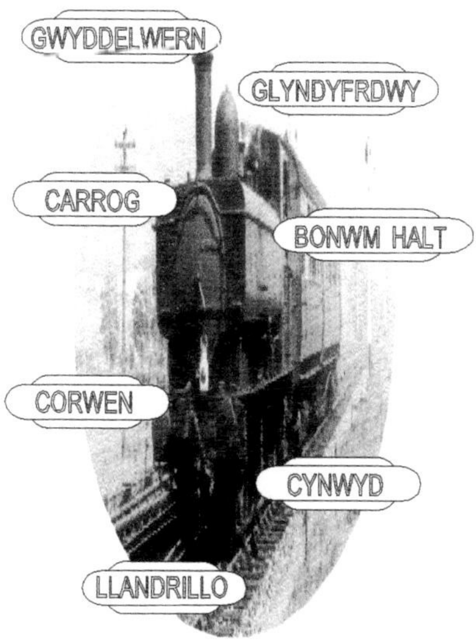

by
Dennis W. Williams

ISBN 0-9540447-0-3

Published by Dennis W. Williams 2001

Rails to Corwen

(A Story of the building of the railway in the Vale of Edeyrnion)

First Published in May 2001
by
Dennis W. Williams
41 Uwch-y-Dre
Corwen
LL21 0BP

Tel: 01490 412563

e-mail: dragoncymru1@supanet.com

ISBN 0-9540447-0-3

Designed and typeset by PCS, Corwen, Wales.
Text typeset in Arial 11pt

Printed by PCS, Corwen, Wales.

CONTENTS

INTRODUCTION i

CHAPTER 1.
BEECHING'S AXE: END OF THE LINE 1

CHAPTER 2.
THE DEMISE OF THE HOLYHEAD MAIL COACH
AND THE CONCEPT OF A RAILWAY LINK
TO CORWEN 10

CHAPTER 3.
ARRIVAL OF THE RAILWAY AT CORWEN
THE DENBIGH, RUTHIN & CORWEN RAILWAY 16

CHAPTER 4.
THE LLANGOLLEN & CORWEN RAILWAY 60

CHAPTER 5.
STATION BUILDINGS 114

CHAPTER 6.
ENGINEERS & CONTRACTORS 141

CHAPTER 7.
NAVVIES 144

BIBLIOGRAPHY 163

INDEX 164

FACTFILE 168

Introduction

The arrival of the railways was a crucial development to the Vale of Edeyrnion and many of the larger landowners became directors of the many companies formed during this period.

In the early 1800's the marketing of agriculture produce in Wales was largely determined by three factors: climatic and physical conditions imposed restrictions on pastoral farming so that the major items of output comprised livestock, wool, butter, cheese and eggs; the absence of large local markets meant that Wales had to export its products; and thirdly, land communications linking Wales with the rest of Britain were so poor and inadequate that coastal shipping was important to the local economy.

The impact railways had on farming was significant. The immediate effect was the reduction in transport costs which subsequently led to the gradual fading out of the droving system. The railway system remodelled the marketing of livestock by influencing the decline of fairs which were held near the railway stations and tended to flourish at the expense of those located at a distance. This was crucial to the economy in Corwen as it brought people and their custom to the town itself as opposed to taking them to other towns and markets. A result of this was that new businesses developed in the town.

The railways also allowed dealers to travel to local farms to purchase cattle and other livestock by way of private sales at the farms. Farmers in the Corwen area as well as other districts, were now able to fatten their animals rather than send them as stores to be fattened near the centres of large demand. This led to better prices for livestock and an increase in employment.

The slate industry also expanded with the coming of the railways and by the mid 1800's it was actually experiencing difficulty in keeping up with the demand of the industrial revolution both for new factories and housing. The railway was now providing not only a quicker method of transporting the slate but also one that was much cheaper, and in the period 1836 to 1882 the tonnage of slates transported increased by almost 30 times (this includes figures for all the North Wales quarries including the much larger quarries of the Ffestiniog district as well as those for the Penarth Quarries).

Although Corwen almost had its first railway in 1845 during the period of the great 'Railway Mania', the first railway to actually arrive in Corwen was the Denbigh, Ruthin & Corwen Railway in September 1864, with the Llangollen & Corwen Railway following in April 1865. It was however in 1860 that the real story begins, when both railways received Royal Assent.

Once this had been granted we would have expected both companies to have pursued the projects with great haste. However, the construction is an episode in itself. We discover the chicanery of one of the contractors whose prevarication delayed the arrival in Corwen of the Ruthin & Corwen Railway.

There is also human tragedy in the building of the railway with the tragic deaths of three navvies on the 'Trewyn Cutting', it later emerging that one person concerned was an Italian with an assumed alias. His was the second fatality and in an uncanny way we discover the details of the third tragic victim, but strangely, no details of the first could be established.

The number of railway casualties during the early years is quite alarming, and the way in which these fatalities are reported in the press is so graphical as to be gruesome to say the least, with scant regard for families of the victims concerned.

With the opening of the Ruthin to Corwen line we unearth a commemorative poem by one of Wales' leading poets as well as the first ever time-table, apparently with a printing error, or were all records shattered with the train travelling from Corwen to Gwyddelwern in one minute? And what of the tree planters in Llangwm in the early 1800's - did they envisage that their saplings would grow to become part of the 'iron road' in the Vale of Edeyrnion some sixty years later? Where would Corwen's station be located? Due to the way in which the river Dee flooded it was envisaged at one time that this would be on its north side and some way out of the town. And who would ever have imagined that a compulsory order on property would be made against the largest landowner in North Wales.

The social and economic benefits of the railway are clearly seen as detailed in reports of a variety of 'Excursions' to the seaside, as well as introducing the people of the Vale of Edeyrnion to the delight of a winter 'Pantomime'. And how else would a slate quarry's 'Brass-Band' travel to perform for one of its owner's?

A consequence of the railway was in increasing volume of transportation. This resulted in almost doubling the numbers employed in the slate quarries together with a welcome reduction in domestic fuel by 43%.

At one time, a scheme proposed a route to connect the Vale of Edeyrnion with a tunnel under the Berwyns, which would see Corwen merely as a branch of the line from Llandrillo.

We also learn of the foolhardy exploits of a prisoner escaping from a moving train in a tunnel whilst on his way back to prison.

Environmentalist's, vandals and trespassers etc., are not modern-day phenomenas, they were around in Victorian times.

It is also ironic that almost a hundred years prior to the closure of the Ruabon to Barmouth railway, we discover details of the '*Great Flood at Corwen*' which immobilised the railway only four months following its opening.

The book itself begins with the end of the line and a brief analysis detailing the closure and some of the grave errors behind it which, while not attempting to absolve the infamous Dr Beeching of 'brutally mangling' the local railway, does at least part remove the horns from his head but perhaps not the axe from his hand.

A considerable amount of the text in this book chronicles events leading up to the opening of the railway to the Vale of Edeyrnion as they appeared in the two newspapers serving the area at that time - the 'Carnarvon & Denbigh Herald' and the Welsh language newspaper 'Y Baner ac Amserau Cymru' (The

Banner and Welsh Times), as well as numerous facts gleaned from a wide number of published books. The statistics on which I draw conclusions are more than mere conjecture, and are taken from the most reliable of sources - Railway returns published in Parliamentary Papers, Inland Transport Statistics and British Rail reports.

The history of the arrival of the railway in Corwen reveals a fascinating account. Relevant to this narrative is the story charting earlier forms of public transport such as the Omnibus coach and that of the Irish-Mail coach which took its route through Corwen from 1832 until 1838.

I make no apologies for the spelling of some place-names - these were as used in the anglicised Victorian period; Dolgelley and Dolgelly for Dolgellau, Carnarvon for Caernarfon etc. The influence of the English influx into Edeyrnion led me to discover the way in which the village of Carrog obtained its name. Indeed, was it pure coincidence or was the fall of soil obstructing the railway line at Carrog in November 1872 Owain Glyndwr's vengeance for this invasion!?

Although the main text of the book concerns itself with the building of and the arrival of the railway in the Vale of Edeyrnion, part of the text does relate to the 20th century when the railway was in its heyday.

I trust that all who take the time to read this book will enjoy looking back into the way the railway arrived in Corwen and the people responsible for its construction and the running of it in subsequent years. All local history is important, and I trust that the contribution of this book will play a small part in bringing some of the history of the railway to all and that it proves to be a source of valuable information to local historians, students and the pedantic. No doubt some readers will find that the book has missed out on several features and items from our past - to those I apologise and trust that they will inform me of such and that at some future date their inclusion may form part of another volume.

Many people have helped with the providing of material and

access to such during the last few years. My wife Pearl has assisted me on all occasions in visiting the Archives in both Ruthin and Dolgellau. I wish to thank Heddwen of the former Clwyd Library Service for the Housebound, to Mr Allan Fletcher in providing me with a comprehensive list of source material, to Mr Elwyn Hughes in providing assistance with the Register of Deaths and Burials in Corwen Parish Church, and to staff at both the Ruthin and Dolgellau Archives and at the Library in Corwen.

D.W.W.

May 2001

"In those days each great invention was granted a lease of many ages in which to foster its own characteristic civilisation before it was submerged by the next; but in our day inventions, each implying a revolution in the habits of man, follow each other thick as the falling leaves. Modern History, beginning from the Britain of 1780, is a series of dissolving views. In each generation a new economic life half obliterates a predecessor little older than itself."

G.M. Trevelyan from 'British History in the Nineteenth Century'.

CHAPTER 1

BEECHING's AXE: END OF THE LINE

From the birth of the railway network 120 railway companies existed in England, Wales and Scotland. The result of this was that railway work was carried on in a variety of ways from good and bad to indifferent. There was no standard pattern for any sort of railway material and no standard practice for any of the work.

The first railway to arrive in Corwen was the Denbigh Ruthin & Corwen Railway in September 1864, with the Llangollen & Corwen Railway following in April 1865. By 1896 the Denbigh Ruthin & Corwen had been absorbed by the London & North Western Railway Company and the Llangollen & Corwen likewise by the Great Western Railway the same year. In 1923 the London Midland & Scottish Railway incorporated the LNWR.

By the Act of 1921 the 120 companies were combined in four groups: the London Midland and Scottish; the Great Western Railway; the London and North Eastern Railway; and the Southern Railway. By 1923 over 9,000 miles of British railways came under the control of these four authorities.

The bringing together of 120 companies into four groups led to more efficient and economical working of the railways. By 1946 the four companies had between them a total of 20,300 steam locomotives, 2283 electric locomotives and rail motor-coaches, 40,856 carriages and 664,914 wagons.

On January 1st 1948, nationalisation of Britain's railways came into being by Act of Parliament. The four main companies were merged into one publicly-owned undertaking with the title "British Railways". The words "British Railways" began to take the place of the companies name on the tenders.

Nostalgia can so easily cloud reality; the past is often recollected by looking through those proverbial rose-tinted spectacles; when making comparisons with what is today and our perceptions of what we believed the situation to be in years gone by, it appears that the 'good old days' have long gone. In this ultra-modern age nostalgia can also prove to be an economic boon. This is often achieved by reviving a past glory of what was once an essential part of our everyday life. In no mean way, railways have played a great part in this modernist revival period and none less so than the Llangollen railway which it is hoped will be extended to Corwen

Table 1: (Revenue from passenger and freight traffic for the U.K)

Year	Miles of lines open	No. of passenger journeys	Population (000's)	Journeys per head of population	Receipts from passenger traffic £000's	Receipts from freight traffic £000's
1841	1,775	11,962	18,534	0.65	2,601	866
1851	6,666	79,740	20,816	3.8	7,197	6,859
1861	9,442	163,042	17,268	7.1	10,967	14,699
1871	13,388	359,673	26,866	13.8	17,146	25,514
1881	15,734	605,404	38,478	20.4	22,760	35,270
1891	17,328	823,262	47,511	24.9	28,548	41,768
1901	18,853	1,145,543	60,762	31.0	44,623	51,235
1911	19,998	1,295,502	64,782	31.7	51,671	61,088
1921	20,299	1,786,671	88,018	41.8	105,853	109,552
1931	20,437	1,606,201	78,593	35.9	78,125	90,451
1941	World War 2		No Census taken			
1951	19,385	1,001,308	51,654	20.5	140,074	227,858
1961	18,240	999,525	54,799	19.5	213,831	236,842
1971	11,655	815,513	69,971	15.1	260,990	258,895
1981	10,831	718,500	66,338	13.2	1,022,800	623,100

No allowance has been made for changes in the value of money.
Sources:
The Railways of Britain, (J. Simmons, Published 1986 by Macmillan London Limited,)
19th century - from Railway returns published annually in Parliamentary Papers
20th century - D.L. Munby, Inland Transport Statistics: Great Britain, 1900-1970
1971-1981 British Rail reports, Annual Reports, 1971, 1981

in the early part of the new millennium. Being part of the old Ruabon to Barmouth route which had served this part of North Wales for the better part of a century, it had - in the words of many a commentator - been brutally mangled by the iniquitous Dr Beeching in 1964. It is widely believed that the majority of railways in Wales during the early part of the 1960's were in a better economical order than at any time since the end of the Second World War. Table 1 on page 2 details the revenue of the railway in comparison to route miles and population.

These figures it must be said are for the whole of Britain as it has proved an impossible task to obtain them for regional areas, especially that of one route such as the Ruabon to Barmouth or the Rhyl to Corwen in particular. However, it can certainly be seen that revenues were increasing if we compare the combined revenue for both passenger and freight per mile of line open (see Table 2).

Table 2: (Combined revenue of passenger and freight traffic per mile of line for the U.K)

Year	Miles of line open	Receipts from passenger traffic £000's	Receipts from freight traffic £000's	Combined Revenue of passenger and freight traffic per mile (£000's)
1841	1,775	2,601	866	1.95
1851	6,666	7,197	6,859	2.10
1861	9,442	10,967	14,699	2.72
1871	13,388	17,146	25,514	3.19
1881	15,734	22,760	35,270	3.69
1891	17,328	28,548	41,768	4.06
1901	18,853	44,623	51,235	5.08
1911	19,998	51,671	61,088	5.64
1921	20,299	105,853	109,552	10.61
1931	20,437	78,125	90,451	8.25
1941	World War 2		No Census taken	
1951	19,385	140,074	227,858	18.99
1961	18,240	213,831	236,842	24.70
1971	11,655	260,990	258,895	44.60
1981	10,831	1,022,800	623,100	151.96

The total route miles had been almost halved between 1951 and 1981 whilst revenue had increased by 800%. It could be concluded from these statistics that the closure plan had been successfully implemented in discontinuing uneconomical routes, but they do not tell the complete story.

What of the revenue from stations located on routes deemed to be uneconomical? The figures in Table 3 details Annual Traffic totals for Corwen station for 1960 which appear to make impressive reading.

Table 3: (Annual traffic totals for Corwen in 1960)

Year	Passengers Booked	Season Tickets	Parcels forwarded	Parcels received	Freight traffic forwarded (wagons)	Freight traffic received (tonnage)
1961	40,000	500	2,000	10,000	1,000	15,000

Source: Railway Magazine (Western Region) December 1961

Without attempting to make too much use of this work as a subject of question or inquiry into the closure of the Ruabon to Barmouth section, nor indeed to absolve Beeching, a closer examination of the consequences of the errors of the 1962 Transport Act along with the decisions taken by the newly-formed British Railways Board and it would not be too difficult to conclude that closure of the Ruabon to Barmouth route was a matter of grave miscalculation made back in the mid 1950's.

The Conservative government's 1962 Transport Act was intended to check the desperate drift of the railways' finances by focussing more management attention on British Railways operations as a commercial enterprise. Thus the all-embracing British Transport Commission was demolished and its London Transport, British Road Services, Docks and Inland waterways constituents were hived off as independent concerns. The railway executive, which had been a subsidiary of the British Transport Commission, was superseded by the British Railways Board, being directly responsible to the Ministry of Transport.

Most importantly, the new Railways Board was given a substantial measure of freedom to pick and choose the traffic it would carry, and to fix its fares and freight charges according to its own commercial judgement.

The historic common carrier obligations were abolished. Another crucial change was that the government shouldered the burden of decision whether to dispense with the loss-making services or to retain them as a social necessity. The British Railways Board could at any time propose for closure any of the services it argued were irretrievable money-losers. The case would be submitted to a new Transport Users' Consultative Committee (TUCC) investigation procedure through which objectors on grounds of hardship could contest the closure at a public enquiry.

The final verdict - and the responsibility for keeping the British Railways Board saddled with the loss if the services were retained - would be with the Ministry of Transport. The nation awaited the first glimmer of financial transformation. But hope faded as the cardinal errors of the 1955 modernization had not been faced. The blatant fault of the 1955 Modernization Plan was its assumption that Britain's economy would stand still for the next 15 years; that the railways could take their time to re-equip and to be able to step back into a competitively unaltered arena and scoop up as of a divine right all the traffic, local and long-distance, passenger and freight, which had been lost to competitors since the end of World War Two. Having being let off the financial leash to embark on a massive re-investment in railways, the 1955 Modernization Plan added up to a capital expenditure of £1,240 million.

A financial reorganization linked with the 1962 Act had

written off £1 billion of British Railways' accumulated losses and debt, which in effect made the new BRB a gift of the railway system, requiring it only to repay with interest what it had borrowed from 1955 onward.

A neatly charted timetable predicted that the BRB would have cleared its slate by 1984. Instead, in its very first year, the BRB slumped a further £76 million into the red. In the spring of 1963 the BRB appalled the country by issuing a 'Reshaping Report' which subsequently became infamous as the 'Beeching Plan', advocating closure of over 5000 route miles of railway and 2350 stations.

Thus it was that Beeching's axe fell on Corwen sounding the death knell on the area's century-long railway link, furthermore delivering a devastating blow to its existing workforce. With the exception of Ruabon to Llangollen, all goods traffic discontinued in 1964. Already earmarked for closure in January 1965, the elements delivered the ultimate cruel stroke on the 12th and 13th December 1964 by way of a deluge causing a breach on the line between Bala and Llandderfel.

Ironically, a century earlier in the August of 1865, four months following the opening of the Llangollen Corwen Railway, a flood caused considerable damage to the railway, on this occasion at Llidiard-y-Park (sic). In complete contrast to the events almost a century on, service was resumed within a few days, the event being reported in the Carnarvon & Denbigh Herald as follows in its edition of 26th August 1865:-

Great Flood at Corwen of August 1865

A few months following the opening of the railway, disaster struck the town of Corwen and its new railway. The newspaper headlined the 'Great Flood at Corwen and Neighbourhood' reported that "On Thursday last this town and neighbourhood was visited by a disastrous flood, second only to the one which took place on the 3rd August 1847 - 18 years ago - and as it is presumed both arose from the same cause, namely, the bursting of a cloud on the Berwyn Mountain. Throughout Wednesday afternoon and night and Thursday morning, the rain fell in torrents but not however, to a greater extent than had often been seen afore. The brook Cawrddu, a mountain torrent when swollen, runs with impetous force through the town of Corwen through a culvert[1] under the houses that are situated on the side of the street nearest the church, and on any occasion when it happens that the volume of water is too great to pass through the culvert it must burst through the floors and the coverings where it can - such was the case on this occasion. About 10 o'clock a.m., the house of Mr Hugh Davies, bootmaker, was the first flooded then the Owain Glyndwr Hotel. A stream of water equal to an ordinary brook was flowing through the front door as well as through all other outlets. Next it broke out at the lane leading to Mill Street then by the entrance to the Church. All the straw and dung from the pards [2], planks of wood and empty candle and soap boxes were called into requisition to prevent the stream, which now poured into the street, from making its way into the houses on the north side. This new powerful stream of water found its way into Mr Moltby's stable yard - thereby flooding his garden - and with difficulty the pigs were brought out of the styes alive.

Business in the town was suspended for the greater part of the day, everybody labouring to keep the water out of their respective premises. At the time of writing, about 5 p.m., the rain having ceased some hours ago, the water has greatly subsided. The places of business are fast assuming their wonted lively aspect and the Owain Glyndwr Hotel appears high and dry.

In our peregrinations along the road to Llangollen, we found much damage to both road and rail. A lot of labourers under the able superintendence of Mr Walker B. C. Jones were clearing the debris which had accumulated near his property, Bron-y-Pigyn and Bron-y-Graig.

The Llangollen to Corwen Railway has been seriously damaged. A culvert which takes away the waters of the Llidiard-y-Park (sic) brook to the Dee was partially swept away, and the water had accumulated in a hollow between the railway and the road. This was flooded to a depth of at least 3 to 4 feet. At Glyndyfrdwy the embankment had been washed away leaving the sleeper quite bare for several yards. It seems that when the train due at Corwen at half past ten was passing this place, the flood was just beginning to attain its full force. However, the careful driver Mr Robinson made his way over and went as far as Carrog with his precious living freight safely. The passengers are now conducted to Corwen in Omnibuses after the arrival of every train from Llangollen.

We found Mr Reid and his assistant Mr Harry Moltby busy inspecting the damage and ably directing a willing lot of navvies to set all right with the least possible delay. Mr Brassey, the eminent contractor of the line, who is on a visit at Rhug, also went over the line during the afternoon, and we have no doubt, with the experience and despatch of these gentlemen, the traffic will be resumed in a day or two".

[1] *I believe this culvert to be that which runs beneath Mill Street and alongside the Bethesda Independent Welsh Chapel.*

[2] *This was the spelling in the C & D H. A definition given in the IBM World Millenium Encyclopedia 2000 CD: (Archaic.) a leopard or panther. Ex. a soldier, Full of strange oaths and bearded like the pard (Shakespeare). Freckled like a pard (Keats). pard (2), noun.(Dialect.) partner; friend; companion. Given the above definitions it may be that it should read yards and not pards??*

Corwen station facade from the west c1900. Photo: Lens of Sutton

Carrog Station - probably the most attractive station building in the Vale of Edeyrnion. Re-named Carrog to facilitate visitors as the village name of Llansantffraid-Glyndyfrdwy was considered too long! Photo: Lens of Sutton

CHAPTER 2

THE DEMISE OF THE HOLYHEAD MAIL COACH AND THE CONCEPT OF A RAILWAY LINK TO CORWEN

In 1797 the London to Holyhead Irish-mail coach timetable took approximately 45 hours. The down coach journey commenced from Charing Cross at 8 p.m.(Day 1) with breakfast being taken at Northampton, dinner at Lichfield and tea at Stafford. At Chester there was a stop of one hour following the scheduled arrival time of 12 midnight (Day 2) to accommodate supper and breakfast being taken, if the itinerary was as programmed, at 5.30 a.m. at St Asaph. The coach passed through Conway at 9.30 a.m. reaching Bangor Ferry House at 12.20 p.m. where an hour was allocated for dinner and the crossing to Holyhead harbour arriving at 4.50 p.m. (Day 3).

Vast improvements to the Holyhead road resulted in a revised schedule being introduced from 5th April 1819 which took 8 hours off the previous journey time. Probably the most famous of all the mail and stage-coaches, strenuous efforts were always made in attempting to improve the journey time. In 1832 the British and Irish Post Offices were amalgamated which added importance to the journey time being reduced. The revised route by this period included stops at Birmingham, Shrewsbury, Corwen and Bangor, and the journey time was down to 28 hrs 6 minutes.

By 1838 a special Act of Parliament had regulated mail to send this particular traffic by trains which marked the end of the zenith of the coaching era. It was perhaps inevitable that sooner or later the Irish Mail would transfer its business to the more economical railway network and thus sever important connections which Corwen played on this route. The surfeit of railway projects which swarmed parliament furthered the cause for Corwen to eventually be placed on the intricate web of railways that was beginning to stimulate the construction of branch lines as well as trunk routes to serve as feeders to main-line undertakings.

CORWEN'S FIRST LINK WITH THE RAILWAYS

Corwen's first link with the railway was probably in 1851 soon after the Padeswood station near Mold was opened at the Ffrith branch junction with connecting road services operating between Mold and Corwen, Bala and Dolgellau. It is worth noting however that the railway almost made it to Corwen in 1845 during the period of the great 'Railway Mania', so called due to the staggering number of proposals in the form of Bills placed before Parliament. Several schemes representing a variety of projects abounded at this time, many of which concerned themselves with re-routing existing railways to reduce distances, especially the route between London and Holyhead. One such scheme was put forward by the London and Holyhead Direct proposing an atmospheric railway[3] departing the Buckinghamshire Railway near Banbury in Oxfordshire to proceed via Stratford, Kidderminster and Bridgnorth to link with the Shrewsbury, Oswestry and Chester Junction at Shrewsbury, then journeying through the Vale of Llangollen to join the North Wales Railway. This initiative, if accepted, would inevitably have brought forward the formation of the Llangollen Corwen Railway. However, it would be a few years before the railway arrived at Corwen.

[3] *atmospheric engine - a variety of steam-engine in which the steam is admitted only to the underside of the piston.*

THE CONCEPT OF A RAILWAY LINK TO CORWEN

The attention of the Government of the day regarding further improvement to the Irish Mail route was occupied for the best part of a decade commencing in the mid 1830's. A railway to London was planned through Meirionethshire, Montgomeryshire, the Teme Valley and passing through Ludlow, Worcester, Stratford and Oxford. The route mileage of 220 miles promised to surpass all others. Following this, the Lord Liuetenant of Ireland commissioned two engineers, Charles Vignoles and John Urpeth Rastrick to survey possible routes from Porth Dinllaen through the North Wales mountains to link with existing railways to the south.

THE SURVEYS OF VIGNOLES AND BRUNEL

Charles Vignoles' most direct route was a trial line taking in Tremadoc, Ffestiniog, Bala, Corwen, Llangollen, Shrewsbury, Iron Bridge and Wolverhampton, giving a total route mileage from Porth Dinllaen to London of 244 miles.

During the period that Vignoles was carrying out surveys covering North Wales, it was reported that the renowned engineer Isambard Kingdom Brunel was surveying a railway route from Gloucester to New Quay on Cardigan Bay. This was envisaged as being a more direct link in a route to Ireland. Despite the many options surveyed by Vignoles in this period, the railway meantime was not to make its way to Corwen. On the 1st August 1859, the Vale of Llangollen Railway Act received Royal Assent; this being the sixth attempt to promote a Bill for a line probing westwards out of the Ruabon-Wrexham area since 1847. The Vale of Llangollen Railway was to leave the Great Western's Shrewsbury & Chester line just south of Ruabon, and had the full support of G.W.R.'s management.

It was not until the summer of 1860 that a number of other projects linked the railway to Corwen. The first real breakthrough came when the Denbigh Ruthin & Corwen Railway received Royal Assent on 23rd July, this following the third reading of the Bill in the House of Lords, and the Llangollen & Corwen Railway was incorporated by the Act of 6th August 1860.

MAP 1

Map detailing routes of the Vale of Clwyd, Denbigh, Ruthin & Corwen Railway and the Llangollen & Corwen Railway.

MAP 2

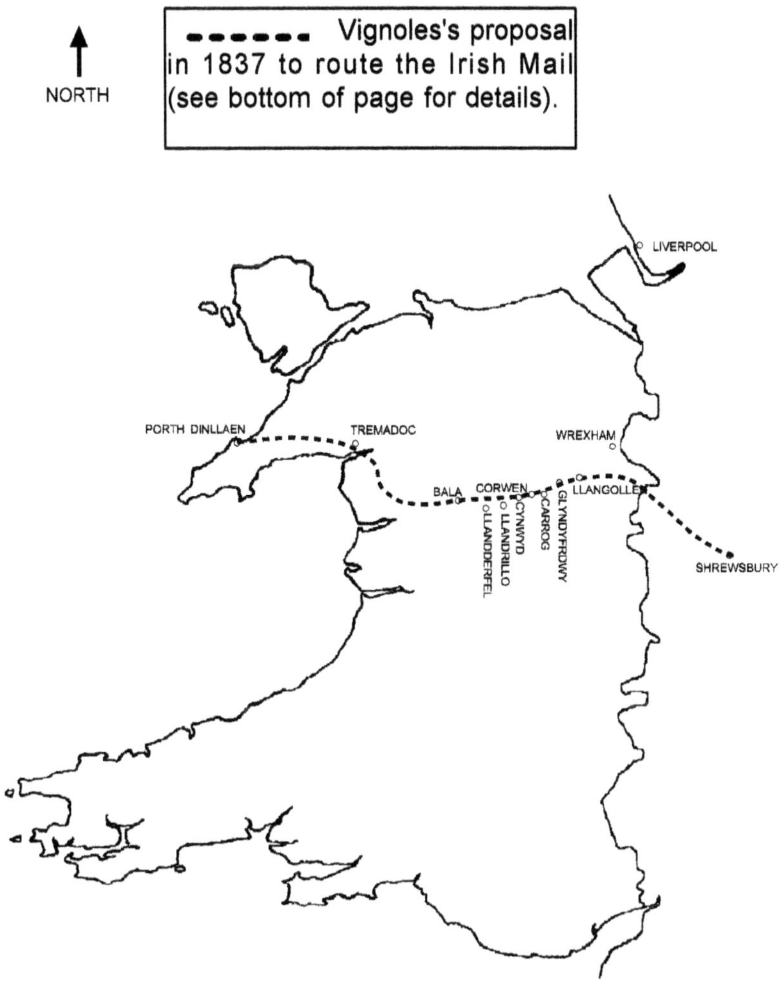

Vignoles's proposal in 1837 to route the Irish-Mail from Porth Dinllaen to London taking in Tremadoc, Ffestiniog, Bala, Corwen, Llangollen, Shrewsbury, Iron Bridge and Wolverhampton, a total route-mileage of 244 miles. This scheme was rejected in favour of the London, Chester and Holyhead route.

CHAPTER 3

ARRIVAL OF THE RAILWAY AT CORWEN
THE DENBIGH RUTHIN & CORWEN RAILWAY

The logo of the London Midland and Scottish Railway Company (LMS).

The Denbigh, Ruthin & Corwen Railway was opened in 1864 and absorbed by the London & North Western Region Railway Company (LNWR) in 1896 and incorporated by the London Midland & Scottish Railway Company LMS in 1923.

There is no record of a logo for the Denbigh, Ruthin & Corwen Railway.

1860

It was on 23rd July 1860 that Royal Assent was received for the Denbigh Ruthin & Corwen Railway and on the 4th September that year, the first sod was turned by Miss Florence West of Ruthin Castle.

Cutting of the first sod (*as reported in the C & D Herald*)

The cutting of the first sod was made by Miss Florence West of Ruthin Castle on the 4th September 1860. A beautifully polished mahogany wheelbarrow and elegant Silver Spade having been presented to Miss Florence West by the Contractors, Messrs Davies and Savin, the Lady proceeded very gracefully to cut the first sod, which she placed in the wheelbarrow, wheeled it along the platform and turned it over at the end. A second sod was cut by Miss Terese West, another by the contractors, one by James Maurice Esq. (Mayor of Ruthin); another by the Father of the Corporation, Peter Roberts Esq. now in his 88th year and formerly Mayor of Ruthin under the old and new Corporation.

It was reported in the C & D Herald as "the first link of a chain of communication with other and important districts has been forged by the hand of a fair lady amid the deafening cheers and congratulations of the inhabitants of the town and surrounding country. In the White Friars Field (Cae Gwynach), where the sod was to be cut, a light and elegant arch was erected under the superintendence of Mr Daniels and Mr Ruckman as a sort of entrance to the large rope-ring bearing the inscription 'Denbigh Ruthin and Corwen Railway' ". The newspaper also carried a report of the large procession including 'A Corps of Navvies, Workmen with their Tools etc.'. Sods were afterwards cut by several others. The line of railway is 18½ miles long and the amount of capital for its construction is £150,300, the borrowing powers amounting to £50,000.

The contractors are Messrs Davies and Savin, whose names are a sufficient guarantee that the line will be made in the shortest possible time, and in the best possible manner. The engineer is Mr Benjamin Piercy, to whom every inhabitant in the Principality must feel under lasting obligations for the exertions he has made in the promotion of railways in Wales.

A collection of stanzas were written especially for the occasion by the celebrated Welsh poet John Ceiriog Hughes [4], and these were then read. One such stanza called 'Yr Agerbair', neu 'Brenin y Ffyrdd' (The Steam Engine, or King of The Road), read as follows:-

Mae'n d'od, mae'n d'od! gwnewch chwithau'r ffordd,
Torwch y tywyrch ar rôs a dôl,
Mae Teyru y Ffyrdd mewn rhwysg yn d'od,
Gyda cherbydiau y byd o'i ol,
Mae'n dda gennyf weled ei anadl gwyn,
Ar odrau'r mynydd a chopa'r bryn:
A chlywed ei chwiban yn galw'n ddigryn,
Mynydd at fynydd, a dyn at ddyn!
Mae'n dod, mae'n dod! os pell yw'r môr,
Agos y dygwydd yr eigron gwyrdd-
Mae llongau'r môr yn dyfod at y ffyrdd.
Benau'r mynyddoedd trwy deyrn y ffyrdd.

Mae'r creigiau'n ffoi i'r pantle draw,
Bryniau a wyriant ar chwith a de-
A chwympa derw hyna'r byd,
Ar ei ddyfodiad mawreddus e'.

Y Berwyn mawr, a'r Wyddfa'r ddewr,
Deimlant yr ebill a blaen y cyn;
O dan eu gwadnau hwyrach daw-
Brenin y ffyrdd gyda'i ddaeargryn.

Chwi ddreigiau'r nos sy'n gorwedd dan
Odrau'r Eryri er's oesau fyrdd-
Fe draidd goleuni trwyddoch oll,

Gyda "Phendragon" mawr deyrn y ffyrdd!
Mae'n dod, mae'n dod! gwnaw'n ninnau'r ffordd-
Ffordd i daranau'r olwynion fyrdd-
A chodwn fanllef un ac oll-
Llwydd i freninaeth mawr deyrn y ffyrdd!

[4] *The bard John Ceiriog Hughes was himself a station-master and in 1872 became the manager of the Van Railway opened in 1871 to transport lead from the Van lead mines in mid-Wales.*

Mr Savin reported that the line between Denbigh and Ruthin would soon be opened and that by 1862 to have it opened to Corwen. At the banquet to celebrate the opening, the Carnarvon and Denbigh Herald reported "The Hall was crowded to excess and a large number could not obtain seats. The collation had been most liberally prepared by Mr and Mrs Green at the County Hall.

1861

Progress of the railway

The C & D Herald reported in its edition of 11th May 1861 that "the works on this line in the vicinity of Ruthin are progressing rapidly. It has been very heavy work as well as dirty for the navvies. The skill of the engineers and the energy of the contractor have overcome the difficulties. A number of men are engaged further on the Corwen line near Ffynnogiau. The recent fine weather has been very favourable for the progress of the work".

A couple of weeks later however, (as reported in the C & D Herald 25th May) at an extraordinary meeting of the shareholder's of the Vale of Clwyd Railway Company (convened under the Wharncliffe Act) held on Thursday last, a Mr Gee questioned the Chairman (Robert Gardner) as to why there was a stop on the construction to Corwen. He looked upon this company as the arbiter of the existence of the Corwen line, but didn't know why it had been stopped, but hoped that the directors would rejoice in the knowledge that the London and North Western Railway Company are likely to be the company to have possession of this railway.

Why then was there a stop on the Corwen line after the report on 11th May suggested that good progress was being made? So often this type of report was given out that if all had been as announced then the railway would have arrived in Corwen by 1862. But once again it proved to be nothing more than a false-card played by the engineers to appease no doubt the desire of the shareholder's who wished to see a return on their investment as soon as possible.

Timber from Garthmeilio for sleeper's

In the July the whole of the larch wood plantation at Garthmeilio, Llangwm, had been felled and sold to Messrs J & E Phillips of Glyndyfrdwy, who in turn have sold it on to Mr Thomas Savin to be used in the construction of the Denbigh Ruthin and Corwen Railway. Little did the planters of the woodland sixty years previously imagine beyond their wildest dreams that their labours would eventually contribute to the construction of the railway heralding the arrival of the steam-age in Edeyrnion.

Although pine became the most widely used timber for railway sleepers, larch was very similar in its composition in that it was on the whole, light and soft, abounding in resinous substances and very durable.

The C & D Herald of 7th September reported on the half-yearly meeting of the Denbigh Ruthin & Corwen Railway which took place at the White Lion Hotel, Ruthin, Mr R.C. Naylor taking the chair. The report was as follows, "In our last report we announced the intention of promoting extensions to Mold and Bala. The main object of the line to Mold was to shorten the distance to Chester, and that of the extension to Bala to place our railway on a trunk-line of communcations between Rhyl and Mold on the one hand, and the West Coast of Wales on the other. We however and our allies succeeded in throwing out upon standing-orders the scheme that was opposed to ours between Corwen and Bala. Matters remain in that respect in the position in which they were this time last year, and such measures will be taken into consideration and adopted as may be necessary for securing our railway its fair share of Merionethshire traffic".

The Engineer's report informed the shareholders that the "works of your railway have made considerable progress in the past six months. Over six miles of railway has been laid between Denbigh and Ruthin and arrangements have been made for a great portion of the land between Ruthin and Corwen, and the work has commenced and possession has been obtained. Your contractor has made all his preparations for putting in hand the whole of the remaining works directly and for prosecuting with vigour up to their completion".

The meeting then terminated, the Chairman observing that Messrs Davies and Savin had got an engine and new trucks with benches at their service to go to Denbigh. About four hundred availed themselves of this opportunity and much enjoyed the trip to Denbigh and back.

A report in the 'Baner' on the 9th October stated that work on the D R & C was completed and that there was much activity on the Ruthin to Corwen section, and if work continued at this rate then it would only be a matter of months before the steam train would be seen puffing its way into Corwen. Once again this over optimism is displayed.

Station at Ty'n y Cefn

A major concern of the D R & C were the numerous river crossings the proposed route would follow from Corwen to Bala, adding considerable to the cost. It was reported that the river Dee at its worst flooding period was an alarming sight which would necessitate raising the level of the railway at least nine feet in order to escape the deluge. To avoid building some six bridges it was pointed out that the optimum route would be on the north side of the valley as this was not only the shortest route, but was also the most even and level terrain.

Originally, the DR&C intended to route the line westwards rather than making the crossing over the Dee and into Corwen, the proposal indicating a station being erected at Ty'n y Cefn. By the middle of November the DR&C reported that the Ruthin to Corwen section would reach Ty'n y Cefn by May 1862.

The proposal to extend the line westwards and locating the station at Ty'n y Cefn were not moved formally but what changed the minds of the railway company not to proceed with this is not altogether clear, almost certainly an economical one, but whatever the reason, the townspeople of Corwen were without doubt spared some shoe leather to make use of the train!

1862

Opening of railway to Corwen envisaged by the end of the summer of 1862

The half-yearly meeting of the shareholders was held at the Lion Hotel, Ruthin, on Friday 14th inst., the Chairman of the board of directors, R.C. Naylor Esq. presided. The Chairman congratulated the forward state of the works. Further discussion ensued on which it was decided that the Denbigh-Ruthin section would open on the 1st March, this being St David's Day would be an appropriate day for the opening of this line. This was only a portion of the line and he thought the better time for the expression of their feelings would be when the line was opened through to Corwen.

He had personally inspected the works between Ruthin and Corwen, and was gratified with the progress made, and he thought there could be no doubt they would open to Corwen by the end of this summer.

At the same meeting, a director's report informed the gathering that "the people of Bala have formed themselves into a company for the purpose of applying to Parliament for the necessary powers to construct a railway from Corwen to their town, and are opposed by parties in the interest of the Llangollen and Corwen Company who are promoting a rival project for a railway from Corwen to Bala.

Believing that the people of Bala are the right parties to take in hand the construction of a railway to that town, and that if made by them, your undertaking will be secured its fair share of Merioneth traffic, your directors have resolved upon giving their support in Parliament to the Bala Company". The report was signed by R.C. Naylor (Chairman).

Again at the same meeting, the engineer Benjamin Piercy reported "That the railway from Denbigh to Ruthin was now ready for public traffic. Further to this, Mr Savin is prosecuting the works with the greatest possible vigour - a great portion of this last remaining section is now ready for the permanent way, the materials for which have been provided and there is every reason to believe that before the end of the summer the whole of your railway from Denbigh to Corwen will be ready for public traffic.

Compulsion Order on property of Rhug Estate

Possession of the whole of the land, with the exception of the Rhug Estate, has been sometime since obtained, and the necessary steps are now being taken for obtaining immediate possession of that land by compulsion. I could not find further details of when this order was implemented.

Opening of the railway from Ruthin to Denbigh

The opening of the line from Ruthin to Denbigh on 1st March, a distance of little more than 6 miles, was an incident of great moment. Captain Johns, in his speech, said "that he had no doubt that with works proceeding rapidly, the line will be open to Corwen before the end of the year".

Some conflicting views and contradictions are apparent here, as at the half-yearly meeting on 22nd February, there was no doubt that the line would be open by the end of the summer, and two weeks later this appears to have changed to the end of the year. But why this prevarication ?

Again the inconsistencies continued, as on May 7th in the 'Baner ac Amserau Cymru' it was reported that optimism was high that the line from Ruthin to Corwen would be opened very soon, and that the contractors, Humphreys and Beckingham [5], were working pulling all the stops out. Quarrying work was also at a maximum on the Berwyn's for stones to build bridges on the line.

[5] *Further confusion arises here as the contractors for the construction of the railway were Savin and Davies, though Humphreys and Beckingham may well have been contractors for bridges and cuttings etc., as the name Beckingham is mentioned in a report of the building of the Trewyn cutting.*

Progress of the Ruthin to Corwen section

The prophecy concerning the opening of the Ruthin to Corwen section was dealt another blow as the year drew to a close with no sign of its completion.

In its edition of 13th December, the C & D Herald reported that the D R & C line is making considerable progress."Our readers are aware that the line has been in full operation from Ruthin since March last, and doing a good traffic. The remainder of this line and stations are all but completed as far as Gwyddelwern. Some little difficulty appears to be experienced in bridging over the Dee at this time of the year, but there can be no doubt the line will be finished and opened through to Corwen early in the Spring".

1863

Half-yearly meeting of the Denbigh Ruthin & Corwen Railway

The Denbigh Ruthin & Corwen Railway Company Directors' Report stated that statements of accounts for half-year ending December 1862 is subjoined and that traffic returns on the line now opened from Denbigh to Ruthin continue to improve. Considerable progress has been made in the works from Gwyddelwern to

Corwen, and it is expected that the whole will be completed and ready for opening early in the ensuing summer.

Benjamin Piercy reported that the portion of railway from Denbigh to Ruthin is in good working order and that the section from Ruthin to Gwyddelwern is now completed, and awaits only the certificate of the Board of Trade to be opened for public traffic.

Of the 2½ miles distance from Gwyddelwern to Corwen, over 1¾ miles of permanent way had been laid and ballasted. The only portion not at present complete is the last mile into Corwen but that the works were in a forward state, the bridge over the Dee being nearly completed and assured by the contractor that the whole of the railway will be completed into Corwen in a few months.

D R & C Railway Company Directors

The list of directors for the company were given in the Caernarvon and Denbigh Herald of 28th February 1863 as follows:-

R. L. C. Naylor, Chairman, John Price, Vice-Chairman, John Jesse Esq., F.R.S., Richard Simpson, Captain Johns, R. G. Ellis, John Jenkins, F. W. Smith, Gabriel Roberts, Oaklands, and Messrs Jones, agent, D. Jones, Green, Roberts and Smart with Mr Wm. Lloyd, Solicitor for the company and Mr George Monsley, Secretary.

Delay in opening to Gwyddelwern

By the end of May considerable surprise was being expressed at the delay in the opening of the railway to Gwyddelwern. It is understood that the line was passed by the Government inspector fully two months ago, and it might have been opened to that place at once. Very many enquiries are being made respecting it, and there is a rumour that a dispute has arisen between Mr Savin the contractor, and the London North Western Company in regard to working the line. The completion of the railway has had the effect of stopping the coach, and there is now no conveyance between Ruthin and Corwen [6] so that the public are worse off than before the railway was made. It is generally hoped that the directors will order the line to be opened without further delay, and so meet the just demands of the country.

[6] *This is baffling as there is no reference to be found of any conveyance between Ruthin and Corwen prior to this, although a Corwen to Denbigh coach was advertised in 1860, but not in subsequent years so that it can be concluded that this must have ceased.*

The Denbigh and Corwen Coach known as the 'Queen of the Vale' departed daily (not Sundays) from Denbigh at 10a.m. on arrival of the Rhyl train, leaving Ruthin at 11 a.m. with arrival time at Corwen scheduled at 12.45 p.m. to meet the Llangollen, Dolgellau and Caernarvon coaches and commencing its return journey from Corwen at 4 p.m. arriving at Denbigh in time for the last trains to Rhyl.

As a result of the delay in the opening of the Ruthin to Gwyddelwern section, a coach service commenced in June 1863 as the following advertisement from the C & D H displayed in its edition of 20th June:-

DENBIGH RUTHIN & CORWEN RAILWAY

The public are respectfully informed that until that portion of the railway be opened between Ruthin and Gwyddelwern, arrangements have been made to convey passengers by Omnibus, in connection with the following trains between the above places.

Leave Gwyddelwern every morning at 7.45 a.m. to meet the Mold coach and the 9.12 train from Ruthin.

Leave Ruthin on the arrival of 3.45 p.m. train.

Rees Powell, Crown Hotel, Gwyddelwern.

No further progress was made towards the latter part of 1863 as it was reported on the 9th December that "It is singular that the line from Ruthin has not yet been opened, it being quite incompleted to Gwyddelwern about 2½ miles from this town. Some months ago, the D R & C Railway Co. drove long balks in front of the pillars of the iron bridge as protection for them by which the soil was much loosened, and by an overflow of the Dee was carried away from about the pillars, leaving great holes and for paving the whole place round the pillars. They have carried 2,000 loads and it is said that they will again have to carry 1,000 loads more. The stones are carried in carts to Tynddol and from there in trucks by rail up to the iron bridge whence they are thrown over promiscuously. A stone bridge is now being built close to Tynddol for the convenience of the inhabitants of the town, to enable them to go into their fields.

The company have not yet settled where the station is to be, there being some dispute between them and the company of the other line (Llangollen Corwen Railway). Such procrastination looks very bad on the part of both parties, but it is hoped that before long they will come to terms and that the railways will soon be completed".

The lattice bridge crossing the River Dee

In early May 1863 the iron lattice-girder bridge spanning the river Dee connecting the embankments on either side, was completed. The 'Baner' reported that it was not certain as to when the railway itself would be constructed, but that it would be some time yet before the whistle of the steam-train would cause a disturbance to the sleep of the inhabitants. The report was pleased to announce that no accident occurred in the construction of the bridge, and now that it was completed, work would comence immediately on the 'Trewyn cutting' on the shoulder of the ancient hill-fort of Caer Drewyn, and that they feared that accidents would occur on this. I'm a little unsure as to why this pessimism, but this could well have grown from experience on similar workings.

Sadly, but true to their predictions, two fatalities had occurred by the end of May. I am unable to establish the first casualty, but the 'Baner', on the 27th May 1863 reports the second fatality occurring on the 23rd May, so we can assume that the first resulted between the date of commencement of the work on the 6th May and the 23rd respectively (see chapter on 'Navvies').

Station - agreement

By the middle of November 1863, the D R & C had reached a settlement with the Ll & C to build a station near to the Calvinistic Methodist Chapel.

The six-span lattice-bridge over the river Dee with a Ruthin bound LMS 2P train crossing over.

In the foreground can be seen the remaining pillar of the footbridge erected by David Davies in 1867. Photo: M. Williams collection

1864

The C&DH carried many adverts for Omnibus routes from and to Corwen connecting with trains at Llangollen. This one appeared in January 1864:-

Llangollen, Corwen & Bala

A well conducted Omnibus runs daily (Sundays excepted) between the above places at the undermentioned hours viz:-

Llangollen	1015
Corwen	1200
Bala (arrival)	1.30
Bala (depart)	2.00
Corwen	3.45

arriving at Llangollen in time for the Parliamentary Trains going to all parts of England.

During the same month a similar advert appeared to convey passengers between Gwyddelwern and Ruthin connecting with trains:-

Coach from Gwyddelwern to Ruthin

That on and after 1st February next, a well-appointed coach will run between Gwyddelwern and Ruthin on Mondays, Wednesdays, Fridays and Saturdays in each week, starting from the former place at 10.00 and returning from Ruthin on the arrival of the 4 o'clock afternoon train.

Proprietor of coach

REES POWELL, Crown Inn, Gwyddelwern.

By May it appears that the Omnibus no longer carried passengers between Corwen and Bala and that starting times had been altered, presumably due to a change in the railway time-table.

Corwen and Llangollen Station

The public is respectfully informed that on Monday 2nd May 1864, an Omnibus will run daily, Sunday excepted.

Leaving Corwen	9.00
Arriving Llangollen Station	10.30
Leaving Llangollen Station	5.15
Arriving Corwen	6.30

The proprietor of the Omnibus was Mr James Moltby of the Owain Glyndwr Hotel.

Arrival of first ever train to reach Corwen

The 'Baner' reported on August 10th 1864 of the arrival of the first ever train to reach Corwen.

"*On Wednesday 3rd August the first ever train to Corwen arrived having made the journey which was required in order to assess the final section of line from Gwyddelwern to the town. A number of wagons pulled a total weight of 150 tons of steel with the structure of the lattice-girder bridge crossing the Dee being the paramount test. The Denbigh Ruthin & Corwen Railway Company were pleased to report that the crossing was made without the least resistance in the bridge. With the timber-structure of the temporary terminus now completed, confidence now ran high as the line awaited only the Board of Trade Inspector's approval prior to being sanctioned with a safety certificate. The enthusiasm however was short-lived as the report on the final stage detailed two flaws on the section; (i) the bridge crossing the road near to Maesgwyn y Felin had cross-timbers that were considered to weak, and (ii) that the bolts on the lattice-girder bridge were weak and would in a short time sink into the timber. In addition to the above defects the report also mentioned the iron bogey which had fallen into the Dee off the bridge near Trewyn.*"

The first Excursions - Trip Rhyl!

Many of us recall those thrilling Sunday School trips to Rhyl, both pre- and post- Second World War, continuing even following the closure of the D R & C in 1952. The Baner reported on the first-ever excursion to make that journey on 1st September 1864:

"*The first ever excursion by railway from Corwen took place three weeks before its opening when approximately 800 people of the district embarked on that momentous day trip to Rhyl.*"

A report in the 'Baner ac Amserau Cymru' stated that "the majority of the excursionists had never before seen a railway let alone experience travel on a train." A week following the opening, the first excursion was operated from Rhyl to Corwen as reported in the Caernarvon and Denbigh Herald and North And South Wales Independent:-

"An excursion from Rhyl and Denbigh on Thursday 29th September brought a great many people to Corwen. The day was beautifully fine and the excursionists, wishing to penetrate further into the country, the carriages, buses, etc., in the town were soon hired by them for Bala and Llangollen, whilst others availed themselves of the beautiful walks up the Berwyn, and along the River Dee. Ample luncheons were provided at the different hotels and inns in the town."

OPENING OF THE CORWEN AND RUTHIN RAILWAY

The long-wished for day at last dawned on Thursday 22nd September 1864 (although many authors incorrectly record this as 6th October). The passenger traffic is conducted by the running of four trains each way every day, and the goods traffic is for the present brought no further than Gwyddelwern. A considerable number of persons availed themselves of the opening day for a trip to and from the Vale of Clwyd.

The auspicious event was celebrated by a public dinner at the Owain Glyndwr Hotel which was attended by the principal inhabitants among whom were the following:-

W. Williams, J. R. Walker, Henry Moser (London), Evan Jones, Rev. E. Owen, Erasmus Edwards, Thomas Jones, Mr Jones (London House), R. Roberts (Tyn-y-Cefn), David Parry, Mr Pritchard (Harp), Morris Roberts, W. Cooke (Liverpool), William Bowdler (Shrewsbury), Mr R. Jones (Surgeon), O. D. Hughes (Solicitor), Mr Jones (National School), Evan Davies (Nags Head), W. Jones (Chemist), D. Roberts (Auctioneer), Mr Roberts (Postmaster), Mr Jackson (Station Master), Mr Lloyd (Draper), Mr Davies (Druid), Mr Evans (Draper), Mr Clarke (British Schools), Mr W. Davies (Queen), Simon Williams (Ty'n Ddol), H. Williams (Police Sergeant), Mr and Mrs Moltby (Owain Glyndwr Hotel).

After the removal of the cloth, the Chairman proposed the usual toasts which were warmly received. The toast of the "Bishop and Clergy of the Diocese" was responded to by the Rev. Mr Owen. The toast of the evening - "Success to the Ruthin and Corwen Railway" was proposed by the Chairman, who expressed the great pleasure he felt at the opening of the railway to Corwen and he hoped the inhabitants would not rest without effecting other improvements at Corwen, and that the subject of the Market Hall already mooted might come to a favourable issue. (The Market Hall and Assembly Rooms - the building now known as Neuadd Edeyrnion - was built in 1887 by the Corwen Market Hall Company Ltd. in commemoration of the Jubilee of Queen Victoria).

Mr Walker proposed the "Town and Trade of Corwen", coupled with the name of Mr Evans, Draper. The toast was responded to by Mr Lloyd, Draper, who alluded to the necessity of having a footpath over the Dee as promised by Mr Savin; more especially as now the railway was opened, the communication is cut off over the bridge. He concluded by calling the attention of the company to this matter, in order that means might be adopted to effect the desired end. The Chairman gave the "Lord Lieutenant of the County, Lord Mostyn", which was duly honoured. Mr Walker gave "the Chairman, Mr Williams," who feelingly returned thanks.

The song (*why not anthem?*) "Hen Wlad Fy Nhadau" was sung by Mr Ashton and Mr R. Roberts after which Mr Moltby proposed the "Ladies of Edeirnion". Mr Williams returned thanks on their behalf.

Mr Walker proposed the "Health of the Host and Hostess, Mr and Mrs Moltby", and Mr Moltby suitably responded.

Those persons who did not avail themselves of the dinner, manifested their gratifications by the "firing of Cannon and other rejoicings". The suggestion by Mr Lloyd the Draper as to the necessity of a footpath over the Dee I believe refers to the fact that when the Denbigh Ruthin and Corwen Railway finally arrived at Corwen, there was no means of conveyance over the Dee apart from the A5 Pont Corwen which crossed the river on the west-side of the town. A footpath near to the lattice-bridge would allow passengers access from the north-side of the river to the station.

Market Hall

Within a month of the arrival of the railway a Public Meeting took place as reported in the C and D H:-

Public Meeting at Corwen

On the agenda at this meeting was the subject of a Market Hall and gas works.

A. W. Edwards of Ruthin stated "*I am an old inhabitant of Corwen and only left it a few months ago, but my affections have not left it yet. I now live in a corporate town and we are now having a Market Hall that will cost £4000. As regards Corwen, have a Market Hall and a Gas Company too, I say. It was said some years ago that Corwen was a Welsh 'Crewe' and it ought to be so; trade will surely run into it if the tradesmen are alive to its requirements*".

We can see here how the railway was already beginning to produce ideas for commercial spin-offs. As for Corwen being a Welsh 'Crewe', this statement is a little ambiguous - does it refer to Corwen with potential as a centre for commerce or a railway junction? - or both?

Time-Table of the Vale of Clwyd and Denbigh Ruthin & Corwen as from 22nd September 1864

	a.m.	a.m.	p.m.	p.m.	p.m
CORWEN		8.08	12.25	3.40*	6.35
Gwyddelwern		8.19	12.36	3.41	6.46
Derwen		8.30	12.47	3.52	6.57
Nantclwyd		8.37	12.54	4.00	7.04
Eyarth		8.45	1.02	4.08	7.12
RUTHIN	6.00	9.00	1.10	4.15	7.20
Rhewl	6.04	9.04	1.14	4.19	7.24
Llanrhaiadr	6.10	9.10	1.20	4.25	7.30
DENBIGH	6.20	9.20	1.30	4.35	7.40
Trefnant	6.28	9.28	1.38	4.42	7.52
St Asaph	6.35	9.35	1.45	4.50	8.00
Rhuddlan	6.45	9.45	1.55	5.00	8.10
Foryd	6.53	9.53		5.07	8.18
RHYL	7.00	10.00	2.05	5.15	8.25

	a.m.	a.m.	p.m.	p.m.	p.m
RHYL	7.40	11.00	4.10	7.05	8.50
Foryd	7.45	11.05	4.15	7.10	8.55
Rhuddlan	7.52	11.12	4.22	7.17	9.02
St Asaph	8.02	11.22	4.32	7.26	9.12
Trefnant	8.12	11.32	4.42	7.37	9.22
DENBIGH	8.20	11.40	4.50	7.45	9.30
Llanrhaiadr	8.29	11.49	5.00	7.54	
Rhewl	8.35	11.55	5.05	8.00	
RUTHIN	8.40	12.00	5.10	8.05	
Eyarth	8.47	12.07	5.17	8.12	
Nantclwyd	8.58	12.18	5.28	8.23	
Derwen	9.05	12.25	5.35	8.30	
Gwyddelwern	9.18	12.38	5.48	8.43	
CORWEN	9.25	12.45	5.55	8.50	

* This must be a printer's error as the journey time from Corwen to Gwyddelwern at this time took between 10 and 12 minutes, and presumably should read 3.30.

N.B. First railway Time-Table from and to Corwen. Reproduced from the Carnarvon & Denbigh Herald edition 8th October 1864 from the Clwyd County Archives and Record Offices, Ruthin.

Competition from Coach-Owners

Shortly after the opening of the line coach-owners may well have seen their share of passenger trade diminishing. The Coach service from Gwyddelwern to Ruthin which departed at 10 a.m. prior to the opening of the railway had by the beginning of October brought forward its departure time to 9 a.m. Although the train departure time was 8.19 a.m from Gwyddelwern with arrival time at Ruthin being 9 a.m., the later start-time of the coach was, I presume, intended to coincide with the departure of the Mold bound coach, presuming therefore that the train time was a little too early for travellers to Mold. The advertisement in the C & D H was as follows:-

Gwyddelwern and Ruthin

A conveyance will leave Gwyddelwern for Ruthin daily, leaving Gwyddelwern at 9.0 a.m. in time for the Mold Coach and leave Ruthin at 5.10 p.m.

Crown Inn, Gwyddelwern.

The departure time of 5.10 p.m. coincided with that of the train service.

There is no reference to the arrival time of the coach at Gwyddelwern, but the train arrived at 5.48 p.m. I'm not too sure as to why the coach departure time was the same as that of the train service, but possible reasons for this was that passengers booked a return ticket, or that the coach offered a little more privacy.

What is puzzling however is that there appears to be this permanent coach service from Gwyddelwern to Ruthin, but nothing appears to depart from Corwen to the Vale of Clwyd. The C & D H does carry an advertisement in 1860 advertising a Corwen to Denbigh service. There is no reference as to where the coach departed from or the route it takes.

Train Services and Time-Tables

In the early days of the railways, no proper time-tables were issued as was explained by Charles Saunders to the Parliamentary Committee on Railways in April 1841; "At the opening in 1838 we found the figures were so inefficient that time-table working was hopeless; one or two engines might keep time, the other eight or ten were always out of time." Modern day commuters would no doubt endorse this as a perpetual problem!

Bridges

On its way out of Corwen the Denbigh Ruthin & Corwen Railway crossed a three -span bridge soon after its divergence

The iron lattice-bridge spanning the river Dee at Corwen built in 1863.

Photo: (J. Roberts & M. Hitches - 'Railways of Clwyd in Old Photographs').

from the Llangollen-Corwen line. The bridge itself was erected to span a gap which allowed access for both farm workers and livestock into fields either side of the embankment.

Another bridge was the six-span lattice girder bridge over the River Dee, each span being 50 feet. The original was a somewhat flimsy structure in appearance with the base of the support piers initially left as a shell but these were later concreted in. At this time only locomotives above Class 5 were permitted to make use of the bridge. Once the bridge had been traversed there was a cutting into the shoulder of the ancient hill fort Caer Drewyn. In the Carnarvon & Denbigh Herald of March 7th 1863, the contractor was named as a Mr Emery.

Between Corwen and Gwyddelwern there was a siding located near to Ty Gwyn which was on the Down side (served by Corwen bound trains). This siding was at one time known as E. Jones & Sons Bryneglwys Siding and used for coal wagons by the Bryneglwys coal merchant between 1904 and 1947.

Footbridge

It must be remembered that at this time there was no means of conveyance over the Dee at the eastern side of the town, the only means of traversing the river being that of Pont Corwen, a bridge leading out of the town on the west side.

At the reception celebrating the opening of the Corwen and Ruthin Railway, a Mr Lloyd (Draper) referred to the necessity of a footpath over the Dee as communication was cut off over the bridge. A footbridge was erected by David Davies in 1867 and one of its pillars can still be seen today from the bridge. The only explanation I can offer as to why the footbridge was considered necessary was to allow inhabitants on the north-side of the river to make their way to the railway station.

Title Deeds dated 19th July 1867 by the Committee of the Corwen Footbridge over the River Dee, to erect, construct and build a footbridge for the sum of £147 are in the papers of Guthrie Jones (Solicitors) at the Gwynedd Archives in Dolgellau.

Savin's chicanery

The main delay of the line being completed to Corwen appears to have been threefold; there appears to have been some chicanery by Thomas Savin, one of two of the main contractors;

there was also the matter of the construction of the multi-span bridge to cross the river Dee as well as the Trewyn cutting. I mention the chicanery by Savin due to its signifance, as approval for the 9¾ mile length from Ruthin to Gwyddelwern had been authorized by Captain Tyler in March 1863. The captain also required that the temporary engine shed which was located over the passenger line at Gwyddelwern to be dismantled, refusing permission to open until this was completed.

Temporary Terminus

Meantime, Thomas Savin had been the recipient of a substantial shareholding as payment for constructing the line and for putting up the initial Parliamentary deposit. The opening, scheduled for May 12th had to be postponed pending a working agreement with Euston. At this time the directors of the Denbigh Ruthin & Corwen Railway were showing interest in leasing the line to the London & North Western Railway, a contingency against the financial interests of Savin in his desire to control the link between the LNWR and the GWR. So what better way for Savin to delay the opening than by unscrupulously completing the work to a standard that would have met the approval of the Board of Trade but not that as demanded by the LNWR to a branch of its railway network. The consequence of this prevarication was that a report approving the remaining 2 mile track from Gwyddelwern to a 'temporary terminus' at Corwen did not appear until August 1864. When eventually the Ruthin to Corwen section was opened, it was to a 'temporary terminus' at Corwen near to the junction with the Llangollen & Corwen Railway.

Savin's downfall

Within a month of the official opening, Savin terminated the leasing negotiations prompting the LNWR to respond that "temporary working of the line by the Vale of Clwyd Company until Mr Savin can find his own stock is carried on entirely at Mr Savin's own risk". Refusing to specify a date for taking over the line, and

Time-Table of the Vale of Clwyd and Denbigh Ruthin & Corwen as from 1st January 1865

	a.m.	a.m.	p.m.	p.m.	p.m.	p.m
CORWEN		8.25	12.50	2.15		6.35
Gwyddelwern		8.35	1.01	2.27		6.46
Derwen		8.47	1.12	2.37		6.57
Nantclwyd		8.54	1.19	2.47		7.04
Eyarth		9.02	1.27	2.57		7.12
RUTHIN	7.30	9.12	1.35	3.05	4.15	7.20
Rhewl	7.34	9.16	1.39		4.19	7.24
Llanrhaiadr	7.40	9.22	1.45		4.25	7.30
DENBIGH	7.50	9.22	1.55		4.35	7.40
Trefnant	7.58	9.40	2.03		4.42	7.52
St Asaph	8.05	9.47	2.10		4.50	8.00
Rhuddlan	8.15	9.57	2.20		5.00	8.10
Foryd	8.23	10.05			5.07	8.18
RHYL	8.30	10.12	2.30		5.15	8.25

	a.m.	a.m.	p.m.	p.m.	p.m.	p.m
RHYL	8.50	10.55		4.10	7.05	8.50
Foryd	8.55	11.00		4.15	7.10	8.55
Rhuddlan	9.02	11.07		4.22	7.17	9.02
St Asaph	9.12	11.17		4.32	7.26	9.12
Trefnant	9.22	11.27		4.42	7.37	9.22
DENBIGH	9.30	11.35		4.50	7.45	9.30
Llanrhaiadr	9.39	11.44		5.00	7.54	Stops*
Rhewl	9.45	11.50		5.05	8.00	
RUTHIN	9.50	11.55	12.05	5.10	8.05	
Eyarth	9.52		12.15	5.17	8.12	
Nantclwyd	10.08		12.25	5.28	8.23	
Derwen	10.15		12.35	5.35	8.30	
Gwyddelwern	10.28		12.50	5.43	8.43	
CORWEN	10.35		1.10	5.55	8.50	

*This train to Ruthin every Saturday night.

N.B. Time-Table reproduced from the C & D H edition 18th January 1865 from the Clwyd County Archives and Record Offices, Ruthin.

on the basis of the engineer's report of the decayed state of the DR&C, notice was given by the LNWR in July 1865 that Vale of Clwyd trains would cease working the line. Subsequently, Savin operated the line from 1st August 1865 with two hired locomotives until he was declared bankrupt the following February, from which time the DR&C took over.

The following January saw James Ashbury, an influential D R & C shareholder take the first step in his mission to remove Thomas Savin's nominee directors. Although most of Savin's team were unseated, two remained as chairman and deputy. Ashbury's campaign continued and by July 1868 had gained full control. This coincided with the opening of the remaining link of the Corwen & Bala and Bala & Dolgelley Railways which substantially increased the traffic on the D R & C. By the Act of 3rd July 1879 the LNWR had gained full vesting powers.

1865

By January 1865 some changes had been added to the time-table as can be seen on page 39.

Corwen Workhouse Board of Guardians and failure to make use of the railway

The old Union Workhouse which still stands today on the London Road housed many vagrants and officials made frequent visits transporting inmates to the 'Denbigh Asylum'. One such incident reported in the C & D H censured the officials for not making use of the railway to convey inmates. The report was as follows:-

Corwen Workhouse Board of Guardians met on Saturday 14th January 1865. Present were Rev. W. Williams Chairman, Rev. R. Roberts, Corwen, Rev. D. Evans, Llansantffraid Glyndyfrdwy, Messrs Morris Roberts, Llantysilio, Thomas Hughes, Llangwm, Edward Humphreys, Llangollen, John Jones, Llanfihangel.

The inmates in the workhouse on the week-ending 4th of January 1865 were 40. A good deal of discussion ensued on account of a charge of £1 . 14s . 8d for car hire and other expenses for the removal of a lunatic from the Workhouse to the Denbigh Asylum. The amount was ordered to be paid, but the officials were strongly reprimanded for not availing themselves of the conveyance by the Corwen Ruthin and Denbigh Railway.

The first trespasser

The 'Trespassers will be prosecuted' signs were familiar to most of us and we observed its warnings most carefully lest incurring a penalty of some £25. In February 1865 the 'Baner' reported on the first person in Corwen to infringe the law of trespassing on railways.

"At Corwen Magistrate's Court an important trial was held. John Davies, Trewyn Fawr, was found guilty of crossing the river Dee by way of the lattice-girder bridge carrying the railway. He was fined the sum of 2s 6d (12½p) and costs as a warning to deter others."

The first vandal

The modern-day phenomena of vandalism is not such a far cry from that of its Victorian counterpart as the following report stated:- "By comparison to the miscreancy of the trespasser, the actions of the perpetrator which caused the derailment of the Denbigh to Corwen train on Saturday 16th December 1865 can only be classed as reprehensible.

The report in the 'Baner' stated surprise that "no one suffered serious injury in the accident which occurred between Llanrhaiadr and Ty Coch cutting at the crossing known as Llwyn. Investigations revealed that stones placed on the line caused the accident and a reward of £20 was immediately offered for information leading to the culprits. This was not the first incident apparently where stones had been placed on the line but it was the first occasion by which such foolhardy behaviour a derailment had resulted."

Gwyddelwern Station showing signs of dilapidation following closure in 1952.

Photos: Lens of Sutton

Within two days a boy, W. Williams, aged 12, had been arrested and remanded in custody for 7 days when he appeared before Denbigh Magistrates.

Having searched publications for 1866 we could not find any follow up to the case, but it would have been interesting to know the outcome as to how vandals were dealt with at that time.

Railway Mania

Railway mania was still evident as in October 1865 there was mention of a railway from Corwen to Mold over the Llandegla moors but nothing materialised.

1866

By February 1866 the journey time from Corwen to Rhyl had increased:-

minimum	0800 - 1010
maximum	1700 - 2025

No reason could be found for this but it appears to be due to a lengthy stop at Denbigh. The Corwen to Ruabon journey time had also increased to one hour.

A number of new advertisements appeared during this year, all these being spin-offs from the Railway, as this one displayed on 30th June.

'Sea Bathing'

With cheap tickets from Corwen to Rhyl at 2s 6d (12 ½ p) return fare.

Already we can see some benefits to the social and economic well-being of the area in that people were able to travel to the seaside on a regular basis although I'm sure that this was much easier for some social groups than others.

This next advert appeared in the edition of 28th July in the C&DH:-

Picnic or Pleasure Parties

From July 2nd to October 31st, 1st, 2nd and 3rd Class return Tickets at Single Fare for the double journey will be issued at all stations on the Denbigh, Ruthin & Corwen railway to parties of not less than 6 x 1st class or 10 x 2nd/3rd Class Passengers desirous of making 'Pleasure Excursions' to places on or adjacent to this railway, the Vale of Clwyd or Llangollen & Corwen Railways; also to Chirk, Ruabon, Wrexham, Gresford, Chester and Shrewsbury and the principal stations on the G.W.R.

The following notice in the C&DH on the 1st September appears to contradict what had been announced previously.

Alteration of Trains September 1866

The 10.30 a.m. train from Denbigh will be accelerated, arriving at Corwen at 11.40 a.m. in connection with the 11.45 a.m. express train to Birmingham, Oxford and London.'

There appears to be some contradiction with the journey time here as the Time-Table of 1865 clearly shows journey-time from Denbigh to Corwen was 1 hour 5 minutes, but now appears to take 1 hour 10 minutes at what is described as 'accelerated'!

On the 8th September the Denbigh, Ruthin & Corwen Railway were advertising:-

'Ten Hours at the Sea Side'.

An excursion departing Corwen at 6.40 a.m. Arriving at Rhyl at 9 a.m. and returning at 7.10 p.m. Arriving at Corwen at 9.30 p.m. Price 2 shillings - Children Half Fare.

Can you imagine what this must have meant to people in the 1860's, 10 hours at the sea-side would be nothing short of 'Paradise' itself! plus the idyllic train journey to boot!

First fatality at Corwen station

The Victorian journalist as we have seen from various reports were often dramatic and graphical in their comments, and this appears to be substantiated in the following report that was in the C&DH on the 10th November, which also at times appears to display an attitude of indifference if not completely insensitivity to the feelings of the working classes:-

Fatal Accident at the Station

"*The greatest consternation was excited at the Corwen Station on Thursday by the instantaneous cutting to pieces of one of the railway servants named Evans on the arrival of the eight o' clock train. The deceased, a young unmarried man, was employed as foreman shunter, but had on Thursday acted as assistant guard, and it appears that while the train was in motion along the front of the platform he attempted to get on the step by the wheels when he missed his footing, went down and was literally torn to shreds. The mangled remains were placed in a box to await the coroner's inquest*".

1867

This letter appeared in the edition of the 4th May of the C&DH, and it clearly shows that passengers were not without their grievances even in these days, and most letters in those days were not accompanied in the press with names and addresses.

The Denbigh, Ruthin and Corwen Railway

Sir,

Permit me through the Herald, to draw attention of the Directors of this railway to the annoyances experienced by those who are under the necessity of travelling by it. In the whole course of my commercial career I never experienced such delays and annoyances as I have recently had upon this line.

Your readers are probably aware that until this last month or two the service of trains on this line (making allowance for its singularly isolated position) was ample. However, now on the eve of summer, the daily service of trains have not only been materially reduced in number, the majority of them are what are called "mixed trains" some of which according to the time bills, travel at the rate of something like 8 ½ miles per hour, but in reality travel at a much slower rate; for instance, a passenger leaving on a train from Corwen a distance of 12 miles, at 8 p.m. may reckon on reaching Ruthin at about 10 p.m.

There cannot be a doubt, but that should the directors persist in providing such indifferent accomodation, the public will be compelled to adopt other routes, and other modes of travelling than that provided by the railway company, and indeed it is rumoured that the old stage coach is about to revive its old operations between here and Mold, with a greater prospect of support than it ever enjoyed. I have not only expressed my own feelings on this matter, but they are those of the whole district, and moreover, the complaints are not only confined to the present unsuitable arrangements of the trains, but I am informed that the inhabitants of the locality are deprived of the usual "excursions" which they enjoyed under the previous management.

In conclusion, I would earnestly express hope, that those who have the management of this line will take such steps as meet the requirements of the public, as only effectual means of promoting the interests and prosperity of the railway.

Yours &c,

Ruthin May 1st 1867. Viator.

As the irate traveller warns the railway company in the above correspondence to the C&DH in May 1867, it is worth noting that as far back as September 1864 there was competition from coach-owners providing a service between Gwyddelwern and Ruthin and Ruthin and Mold.

This letter to the C&DH from the Railway Times appeared in the edition of October 5th, and relates to the Denbigh, Ruthin and Corwen Railway Company:-

We are indebted to the Carnarvonshire & Denbighshire Herald for the report of the proceedings at the meeting of this company. The main characteristics of which appear to be, first, a cold stolidity on the part of the chairman not to perceive that he and his colleagues stand in the way of improvement and second, a firm determination on the part of Mr Ashbury not to be content with the exceeding candour or condescension of the directors to accept or to act on the advice of others so only that they be permitted to retain their seats. It must be amusing to those at least who have no personal or pecuniary interest in the concern, to witness the want of apprehension on the part of result either from inquiry, or from the introduction of new directors when those still in office represent themselves as prepared to do anything which, to them or to anyone else, may be suggested as beneficial to the undertaking - saving and excepting, of course, the unpalatable proposal of resignation. On the other hand proprietors generally will be glad to perceive that the leading influences represented by Mr Ashbury, while determined to probe the past history of the company to its very core, are not disposed to do so in a manner too common with committee of investigation. Instead of representing a merely speculative or of being animated by a sordid desire to carry out their own views at whatever cost, the committee appointed at the meeting last week will be found representing the greater bulk of the capital as well as acting on behalf of one and all of the separate interests which might otherwise have been left to drift into antagonism.

The private ends of jobbing contractors and more especially the effort to foist the Mold & Denbigh on the Denbigh, Ruthin & Corwen, must not merely be checked, but exposed. The extreme folly of waging war with the London and North Western on behalf of schemes even in a more desperate condition than the Ruthin and Corwen itself must be exhibited in its true colours as well as its inevitable results. And as we feel confident will be the case, should the committee, which has already commenced its investigations, not alone into the actual conditions of the line, but into the charges that have been made for its construction, maintenance, and its management, deal strictly, but not sternly, with every matter that may be brought under its observation, and should the company thereafter be placed under the control of a board properly and efficiently responsible to every class of its owners, there will be more than solid and hearty thanks to Mr Ashbury for his effective yet dispassionate interference, by which alone the property can be saved from irretrievable confusion.

1868

The following report was in the C&DH 13th June edition

Half-yearly meeting of the Denbigh, Corwen and Bala Railway Companies

Half-yearly meeting of the Denbigh, Corwen and Bala Railway Companies held on 28th May reported that revenue from all sources amounted to 5500/-, an increase of 650/- over the same period of 1866. This was due mainly to an increase in passenger traffic now that the line was open through to Bala. Lack of shed accomodation led to exposure from weather causing damage to some carriages, but the permanent way was in good order excepting some sleepers which have to be replaced due to decay.

The company was at this time facing financial difficulties and a receiver of the earnings of the line had been appointed by the Court of Chancery.

The directors would endeavour in the next half-year to prepare a scheme of arrangement under the Companies Act 1867 by which the present proceedings in the Court of Chancery may be terminated, and this they feel to be the only course of action to place the company on a sound footing.

1869

There were no reports in 1869 for the Denbigh, Ruthin and Corwen railway.

1870

In reading the following report that appeared in the C&DH in October there is no denying anyone a chuckle, but looking deeper into the matter there are so many similarities to the railway of today, and the perception you have is that the problems that persist today have perpetuated over the years:-

"*desiring to call attention of its readers who may find themselves unfortunate victims should their luggage be, by accident, mislabelled to a station otherwise than their destination, and on application for it upon arrival, the railway officials will not only delay forwarding it, but charge the unfortunate victim for such detention of the luggage*".

The correspondent also claims that if you are in danger of losing a train and therefore too late to purchase a ticket for the said journey, the order of the railway company is to the effect that "*when the passenger arrives at his/her destination he is subjected to some fearful interrogation*".

A Poem from 1870

This poem was discovered in the archives at Ruthin.

The Railway Platform

Now out they come, a various crowd,
With carpet bags, and laughter loud,
While babies squeal, and porters shout,
And all press onward to go out.

Unfortunately, no details were discovered regarding author's name.

Time-Table

The Time-Table from Corwen to Denbigh in October 1870.

Time-Table of the Denbigh Ruthin & Corwen Railway

Corwen to Denbigh - October 1870

	a.m.	a.m.	a.m.	p.m.	p.m	p.m.	p.m.
CORWEN		7.50	10.35	1.30	4.50	5.40	8.10
Gwyddelwern		8.00	10.45	1.40	5.00	5.50	8.20
Derwen	8.10	10.55	-	5.10	6.00	8.30	
Nantclwyd		8.18	11.00	2.00	5.15	6.08	8.35
Eyarth		8.30	11.10	2.15	5.25	6.20	8.45
RUTHIN	7.40	8.45	11.15	2.45	5.30	6.30	8.50
Rhewl	-	8.50	11.25	2.50	5.35	-	8.55
Llanbedr	-	8.55	11.30	2.58	5.40	-	9.00
DENBIGH	8.10	9.10	11.40	3.10	5.50	-	9.10

1871

Reporting on the 18th March on the personal cost to themselves, it appears that railway companies presumed personal exoneration with monies paid out by way of insurance:-

The cost of railway accidents

It is some small satisfaction to know, remarks the "Lancet", that railway companies do not maim, mutilate and kill their passengers gratuitously. During the past year a total sum of 333,715/- was expended by railway companies in the U.K. It would be interesting but impossible, to collect particulars as to the injuries inflicted upon their victims, whose hurts were supposed to be healed by the application of more than a quarter of a million pounds of money.

The following report which appeared on the 15th April, again highlights the social as well as the economic benefits of the effect the arrival of the train had on the community.

Excursion Trip

The new brass band belonging to Penarth Slate Quarries, Corwen, made an excursion on Easter Saturday, down the Vale of Clwyd and were very hospitably entertained at Plas Clough, Denbigh by J. Parry Jones Esq., one of the proprietors of these flourishing quarries. The band attired in their handsome new uniforms, reached Denbigh station at about 11.30 a.m. and proceeded to Plas Clough. There they played several pieces in good style. They afterwards sat down to dinner at which Mr Parry Jones presided, with Captain J.C. Wynne Edwards in the vice-chair. After honouring the loyal toast, and several good songs had been sung, the company went into the garden where the band again played a selection of airs. Before leaving Denbigh, a visit was taken to the fine old ruins of the castle and its gymnasium, and in due time a start was made homeward, all very pleased with their days enjoyment.

How else could this pleasure trip have been made other than by train?

Having mentioned the social and economic benefits of the train to the area's well being, the following report in the same edition brings to the fore one of the many tragic accidents that occurred in the early years of the railway.

Ruthin Inquest

On Good Friday an inquest was held by Dr Pierce, Coroner, touching the death of Margaret Jones, aged 81, who was knocked down when crossing the Denbigh, Ruthin & Corwen Railway line by an engine on the previous day. The engine driver a Mr Watson, the guard and fireman were examined, and it appeared that they were with the train which ought to have left Denbigh at 4.15 p.m., but for some reason did not start for some nine minutes later after the appointed time. The old woman was noticed to enter the wicket gate to cross over. Had she continued she would have passed safely enough, but she appeared to consider for some time until the train was within 30 yards from her, and then she ran across. The engine was quickly reversed just as she crossed the second rail, the buffer of the engine struck her, and threw her right to the side of the line. The train was stopped, and the deceased taken up, and attended to by Dr Jones of Ruthin, who happened to be in the train, but life was found to be extinct. It was evident the poor old woman had no business at the place, and a verdict of accidental death was returned. But a presentment was signed by eleven of the jury, recommending that a foot-bridge should be made over the crossing by the railway company.

1872

Similar to 1869, there were no reports in 1872 for the Denbigh, Ruthin and Corwen railway in any local newspaper.

1873

In the July complaints were received by the Denbigh, Ruthin & Corwen Railway Company, stating that the railway communications between Rhyl and Ruthin and Corwen had deteriorated.

Previously it was said that visitors to Rhyl could remain at the seaside until 9 p.m., but under existing arrangements they had to depart at 6 p.m., therefore being deprived of three extra hours at the pleasantest time of day.

It was hoped that the Traffic Manager, a Mr Cartwright, would restore the 9 p.m. train.

1874

Again nothing was found for 1874 relating to the Denbigh, Ruthin and Corwen railway.

1875

The Corwen news section of the C&DH on the 7th August 1875 reported a famous name of that period visiting the town:-

Mr Moody

This well-known American evangelist visited the town on Monday 26th July and was recognised by several people who happened to be on the railway platform.

On researching the Encyclopaedia Britannica 2000 CD-ROM, I found reference to a Dwight Lynam Moody, born in East Northfield, Mass., U.S.A. in 1837, worked on his mother's farm until he was 17, then left to work in Boston. In 1860 he gave up business for missionary work which involved the Y.M.C.A. In 1870 he became noted for contributing to the growth of the 'gospel hymn' and made extended evangelical tours in Great Britain (1873-1875 and 1881-1884).

This appears to tie-in with the report. Mr Moody I presume must have been the 'Billy Graham' of the Victorian era.

1876

In the July, notice was given in the C&DH regarding cheaper rail travel.

Railway arrangements

Great improvement has been made in the train service upon the Denbigh, Ruthin and Corwen line this month, and cheaper facilities have been given to visit Rhyl, whilst return tickets at a low rate are now issued to Barmouth.

The month of October witnessed another fatality at Corwen railway station as the following report reads:-

Another tragedy at Corwen railway station

A painful illustration of the danger of attempting to enter a moving train, was shown at Corwen railway station on Monday evening last. It appears that a fair was held in the town on the day in question and owing to the crowd, there was a great crush and scramble at the station. Mr William Owen, watchmaker, in attempting to enter a carriage when the train was in motion, fell under the wheels and received frightful injuries. The unfortunate man died fifty minutes after the occurrence.

Navvy's widow dies

In the chapter on Navvies it was reported that three men had died during the construction of Trewyn cutting, but unfortunately only the name of the second man killed (Black Tom) could be established, as the first and third were not to my knowledge ever reported, only the fact that when the second tragedy occurred was the first one mentioned. This following report on the 11th November however throws light on the name of the third victim:-

Death in a Wesleyan Chapel

The inhabitants of Corwen were painfully excited by the report of Jane Williams (widow of Morris Williams, who was accidentally killed on the Trewyn cutting of the Denbigh, Ruthin and Corwen Railway some years ago) had suddenly died in the Wesleyan Chapel of which she was a member. On Sunday week, the deceased went to the singing meeting which is held before the evening service, apparently in good health, and whilst singing she was seen to fall. On being raised she was found to be dead. Great sympathy is felt in the neighbourhood for her family in their bereavement. The cause of death is supposedly heart disease.

The funeral took place on Wednesday and following at the Corwen churchyard, and was attended by a large concourse of people.

The following report on the 30th December appears to reinforce that more value was placed on rolling stock than on human tragedy.

Cost of Railway Accidents

The various railway companies paid as compensation for injuries to passengers during last year was no less than £381,038, being an increase on the previous year of £25,162. In 1871, £312,334, in 1872 £299,389, in 1873 £364,501, in 1874 £251,293 and in 1875 £278,917. But these amounts do not represent the total cost of accidents on railways. They do not include the cost of repairs to the rolling stock or to the permanent way and works or the deterent influence (which is sometimes considerable) on passenger traffic, but the damage to goods on account of which compensations are paid are not, on the other hand all the results of accidents.

1877

Railway Accidents

In the February, the 'Blue Book', presumably a report of the Royal Commission on Railway Accidents, concluded that most of these so-called accidents are preventable. It reported a long list of disasters for the year 1874 in which 80 passengers and 46 employees were killed in train accidents alone, exclusive of the 742 railway workers/servants and 556 other persons killed in stations and on the line. The report continued saying that many railways were in a ruinous and totally unsafe condition. Also under scrutiny in the report was the criticism levelled at unpunctuality of trains.

Passenger sues LNWR

In March a report in the C&DH stated that a passenger was awarded the sum of 8s/6d (42 ½ p) having sued LNWR for unpunctuality of a train in arriving 45 minutes late. Not a princely sum, but certainly a principle to be adopted in this modern era with the chaos of the modern day network of errors.

1878

The age of the train continued bringing advantages to the local economy as the following report in the C&DH on the 31st August showed:-

Discovery of Slate

Two slate quarries are being opened out at Melin-y-Wig and Derwen on the Ruthin-Corwen line. It was reported that the quality of the slate is good.

This appears to be in contrast to what was occurring in the main slate quarrying areas of North Wales, as there was much talk of depressions and reports of reduction in wages. One problem appeared to be that the size of the slate was too small, but also the resolutely respectable quarrymen of North Wales were experiencing a desperate struggle to win recognition for their union against the neanderthal Lord Penrhyn.

LNWR Take Over

It was reported that since the Denbigh Ruthin & Corwen line was taken over by LNWR, the number of passenger services had decreased.

Unfortunately, I cannot find any time-tables of this period to make comparisons.

Street Lighting

This report in September on street lighting appears to be acting on the demand of rail passengers:-

The gas authorities have determined to double the numbers of gas street lamps for the coming winter. These lamps were few and far between, new ones are to be concentrated around the Corwen railway station, so we trust that the inhabitants of Corwen will have no cause to complain on this subject in the future.

In October it was announced that *"the London and North Western Railway Company are erecting a new telegraph line between Denbigh and Corwen. We understand that the government service will be transacted through this channel, and the old rail line will be done away with."*

1880

The papers are devoid of any reports for the year 1880. Not even any time-tables are made available.

1881

The following report in January announcing what appeared to be the first annual dinner of railway employees.

Railway employees' annual dinner at the Eagles Hotel.

Including guests, over 100 sat down to partake of the splendid repast.

The C&DH also reported during the same month that many railways were blocked due to heavy snowfalls.

1882

Pantomime

We have seen over the period since 1865 how the railway was beginning to transform peoples' lives. It was providing direct employment for dozens of people in the area as well as allowing small businesses to develop. In addition to all this it allowed people easier access to various parts of the country. How many people in the Vale of Edeyrnion had ever seen a pantomime prior to 1882? The following advert on the 28th January was now making all this possible, although I'm sure that the vast majority of the working-classes were unable to make the excursion, especially as this involved a three day stay in Liverpool.

LNWR

The LNWR were advertising '***a three days in Liverpool excursion***' to enable passengers to visit the various pantomimes.

Fare from Corwen: 5 shillings (25 p) return

It offered further concession by way of reduced charges to theatres for those who had travelled by train. These were shown as follows:-

THEATRE	GALLERY	PIT	SIDE BOX	DRESS	STALLS
Prince of Wales	6d (2 ½ p)	1s (5p)	2sh (10 p)	5sh (25 p)	4 sh (20 p)
Royal Court	"	"	"	"	"
Hengler's Cirque	"	"	"	"	"

Hague's Minstrels,)
St James' Hall)Half-price to any part of the Hall except the Gallery.

Bather's Tickets

In the July, the LNWR were introducing issuing of cheap or bather's tickets from Corwen, Ruthin and Denbigh to Rhyl and will continue to do so during the summer months.

Though this had been a practice of the past years, it was noted that the issue of tickets this year were later than in previous years.

CHAPTER 4

THE LLANGOLLEN CORWEN RAILWAY

1860

The original Llangollen to Corwen run, approximately 10 miles in length, was opened on 21st April 1865, and not on 8th May as widely believed (see Carnarvon and Denbigh Herald 29th April 1865). It was built and worked by Henry Robertson the engineer who was also the Member of Parliament for Shrewsbury, and Messrs Thomas Brassey and Field the contractors (Brassey, a phenomenal organiser by all accounts, undertook the construction of 1700 route miles of British railway).

Logo of the Great Western Railway

The Llangollen & Corwen Railway was opened in 1865 and absorbed by the Great Western Railway Company in 1896.

There is no record of a logo for the Llangollen & Corwen Railway.

It must be presumed that as there is no record of the proverbial ceremony of 'the cutting of the first sod' of the Llangollen Corwen Railway, that the ritual performed for the Vale of Llangollen Railway by the wife of Colonel Tottenham, the chairman, on 1st September 1859 sufficed to serve that of the former, although, as previously stated, the Llangollen & Corwen Railway only received Royal Assent on 6th August 1860.

Earlier in 1860, on Thursday 5th April at the Vale of Llangollen Railway half-yearly meeting, it was reported that the Bill for making a railway from Llangollen to Corwen had passed the House of Commons, and that it was expected that the whole of the line would be opened by early 1861, (although eventually not opened until 1865).

By the 4th August at the General Meeting of the shareholders held at the Town Hall, Llangollen, the Chairman, Charles J. Tottenham, reported that the Act for the Llangollen to Corwen Railway is now only awaiting Royal Assent, and that the railway, in conjunction with the Denbigh Ruthin & Corwen Railway, united to the Vale of Llangollen Railway, will form an important through communication into the Vale of Clwyd.

It is interesting to note that by August newspaper adverts appeared offering insurance for travellers. The following advert appeared in the Carnarvon & Denbigh Herald on Saturday 18th August 1860:-

Railway Passengers Assurance Company, 3 Old Broad Street, London, claimed that 1 in 15 of those insured were injured yearly by accident of some description.

The Meirionethshire Schemes

Towards the end of 1860 a series of Public Meetings were held in both Corwen and Bala to discuss a variety of projects. It was proposed to link Thomas Savin's Denbigh Ruthin & Corwen Railway with a Corwen Bala & Barmouth Railway enabling a further link with the projected Aberystwyth & Welsh Coast Railway. The G.W.R. were intent on a take-over of both the Denbigh Ruthin & Corwen and the Vale of Clwyd lines which would succeed in taking it to Rhyl, and at this time had no proposed scheme west of Corwen.

Opposing the Corwen Bala & Barmouth Railway, the West Midland Company, making attempts for a merger with the G.W.R., brought forward the West Midland Shrewsbury & Coast of Wales proposal. This proposed route would connect Shrewsbury to Llanymynech, where junctions would make further connections to the Oswestry & Newtown line and the Porthywaen branch, then progressing via Llangynog and a 1½ mile long tunnel under the Berwyn mountains to Llandrillo. A branch-line at Llandrillo would connect with Corwen and westwards via Bala and Dolgellau to connect with the coast at Barmouth, Harlech and on to Porthmadog.

The prospectus further emphasised the urgent demand of manufacturer's in the West Midlands to have access to sea-ports. A bi-functional scheme would allow the slate products of North Wales to be transferred on the eastward run whilst allowing coal and limestone from the West Midlands to come west into Mid and North Wales.

The preliminary prospectus was placed in newspaper advertisements including the Carnarvon & Denbigh Herald on 15th September 1860 as follows:-

WEST MIDLANDS, SHREWSBURY AND COAST OF WALES RAILWAY

Preliminary Prospectus highlighting the urgent demand for a direct outlet from the mining and manufacturing districts of Staffordshire, Worcestershire, Warwickshire and Shropshire to the sea-coast. The line will commence by junctions with the Shrewsbury and Welshpool and Severn Valley Railway and will pass through rich agricultural districts of Ford, Cardiston, Rowton, Alberbury, Shrawardine, Ensdon, Nesscliff, Kinnerley to Porthywaen and crossing the Oswestry and Newtown Railway.

At Porthywaen and Llanymynech is an inexhaustible supply of lime of superior quality. From thence the line will will proceed near Llanfyllin and Llanrhaiadr to Llangynog.

The line will be carried through the Berwyn Hills to Llandrillo from whence a branch will be thrown out to Corwen, at which place it will join other lines already authorised.

Burchells (Solicitors)

5 Broad Sanctuary,

Westminster,

R.S. FRANCE

SHREWSBURY, (SECRETARY)

The scheme was eventually withdrawn, due mainly to the fact that the West Midland company would have 44 miles to connect Corwen, and consequently the Corwen Bala and Barmouth line was favoured. Influential in this progress was Colonel Tottenham who supported the Corwen Bala and Barmouth Railway, and in turn Paddington supported the Colonel and subsequently Thomas Savin lodged a Bill for a Denbigh Ruthin & Corwen link to Bala which was eventually refused.

Corwen to Bala Railway

Despite Thomas Savin's prediction that the Denbigh Ruthin & Corwen Railway would arrive in Corwen by 1862, it would in fact be a further four years before this transpired. But already plans were in hand to extend the railway from Corwen to Bala. The 'Baner' reported a meeting at the Lion Hotel, Bala, on Tuesday 2nd October 1860 to discuss proposals by the D R & C Railway. The chair was taken by a Mr J. Jones, Fachddeiliog, and Mr

Thomas Piercy the engineer, in outlining the proposal, reported that the West Midland Railway would be pressing hard for their scheme. The feeling of the meeting was in favour of Mr Piercy's proposals but that it would be best to await the outcome of the meeting planned for October 16th which would have present the head personnel of all three interested companies.

Following on from the meeting held at Bala on October 2nd, a number of people assembled at Dolgellau during the morning, and the report continues that "never had so many rich and influential people of the county convened together." The two proposals put forward were the West Midland Railway Company and that of the Welch Coast Railway who were in consultation with the Llangollen to Corwen Railway. Following a heated discussion lasting over 3 hours, the meeting concluded in favour of the prospectus of the West Midland Railway Company as this would appear to be the one that would be most advantageous to local businessmen.

The same evening a further meeting was held at Bala where once again the companies submitted a draft of their proposals. The West Midland Railway's proposal would branch the line from Shrewsbury to Porthmadog via Hanwood, Porthywaen Lime Works, Llangynog, Llandrillo, Bala, Dolgellau, Abermaw, Harlech, Porthmadog and connecting to Porth Dinllaen. At this time there was no suggestion in their submission of a branch from Llandrillo to connect up with Corwen.

The second proposal by Mr Thomas Piercy on behalf of the D R & C Railway would extend the line from Corwen to Bala via Cynwyd, Llandrillo and Llandderfel and connecting through to Barmouth. At Barmouth it would connect with the 'Coach Line' that was proposed to connect Porthdinllaen with Milford Haven.

In presenting the third proposal on behalf of the Llangollen Corwen Railway, Mr Henry Robertson was unsure at this moment in time as to whether his route would reach Bala via Edeyrnion or Bethel and on to Porthdinllaen via Ffestiniog.

The meeting closed by concluding that it was far too early to reach any decision on the three proposals submitted until further enquiries had been made prior to convening another public meeting.

During October, the correspondent for the 'Baner ac Amserau Cymru' reported that there was much talk in the area concerning the two railways which had now received Royal Assent to be constructed as well as the proposed plans to extend the line to Bala. One of the proposals planned to take the route via Dwyryd and Bethel with the second proposal to direct it through the vales of Edeyrnion and Penllyn.

Railway from Corwen to Bala

On Friday 5th October a public meeting was held at The Owain Glyndwr Hotel at Corwen, which had been convened by the promoters of a line of railway from Corwen to Bala. A considerable number of inhabitants of the town and neighbourhood were present, and Dr Walker was voted to the Chair. The promoters of the proposed line were:- Mr G. H. Whalley, M.P., Captain Johns, Mr Piercy, Mr Hardwick (London), Mr George Lewis (Oswestry), Mr Thomas Jenkins, Mr John Jenkins and Mr R. Ellis (Ruthin). Colonel Tottenham said he had listened with a great deal of pleasure to the proposal of Mr Piercy for making a railway to Bala. However, whilst he was anxious to see a railway to Bala, he thought care should be taken in laying out the line to Bala in such a manner as to facilitate an ultimate extension to Ffestiniog. He thought it mattered very little whether the Denbigh Ruthin and Corwen Railway or the Llangollen Corwen Railway extended to Bala.

Half-yearly meeting of the Llangollen & Corwen Railway

On Monday 29th October, the first half-yearly meeting of the

Llangollen & Corwen Railway Company was held at the Town Hall, Llangollen. The directors reported to having the satisfaction of reporting that the company was successful in their application to Parliament for an Act to construct the Llangollen and Corwen Railway. The Great Western Railway are prepared to enter into working arrangements with the company.

They also recommended that Mr Pratchett of Shrewsbury and Mr Edwards of Corwen, be appointed auditors at a salary of 10 shillings per annum.

Local farmer's voice their concern

As plans unfolded in both the press and by word of mouth concerning the routes of the railways, the 'Baner' reported on December 19th 1860 that "*many an old farmer voiced their concern that the Corwen to Llandrillo Railway would route its way through the best agricultural land*". It appears farmers were preparing a contingency to potential low prices for land in view of the poor year for railways resulting in a meagre return for shareholders.

At the same time some joy was envisaged that the arrival of the railway would see a fall in the price of coal haulage which subsequently it was hoped would see a reduction in domestic prices which locally were 1shilling and 2d per hundredweight.

1861

A comparatively quiet year in 1861 for the Llangollen Corwen Railway except that amongst the Bills read in the House of Commons on the 7th February was that for the Merionethshire Railway. Mr Thomas Piercy advised that there was very little opposition against the Bill for the Corwen to Bala Railway.

1862

St David's Day and the cutting of the first sod of the Berwyn Tunnel of the Llangollen Corwen Railway

The Annual Dinner in commemoration of St David's Day will take place on Monday 3rd March 1862 at the Royal Hotel, Llangollen, and the same will also be held in honour of the commencement of the Berwyn Tunnel.

Henry Robertson Esq. in the chair, Mr Ellis Roberts, Harpist to His Royal Highness The Prince of Wales has been specially engaged for the occasion.

The sod cutting will take place near the county boundary in the parish of Llangollen at 1 o'clock p.m. and the dinner will be on the table at 5 p.m.

It appeared at this time that the Llangollen Corwen railway would be ready sooner than expected as the 'Baner' reported that four men and one wheelbarrow had been seen working in the vicinity of Bwlch Rhisgog since March 1st, and that the Berwyn Tunnel was expected to be completed in the near future. This buoyant mood was surely transitory as March 1st marked the event of the 'cutting of the first sod of the Berwyn Tunnel' and to expect four men and a wheelbarrow to tunnel 686 yards of earth and rock on a sharp curve and incline would be to imagine and expect nothing short of a miracle!!

The Berwyn Tunnel (Bwlch y Rhisgog) from the Glyndyfrdwy side.

Drawing by D. Williams

Towards the end of June news reached Corwen that 'tunnellers' working on Bwlch y Rhisgog had come out on strike for more pay, and consequently approximately 100 navvies had arrived there to take over the work.

Savin's downfall

Once again further proposals were put forward, notably Savin's Bala Railway and the Meirionethshire Scheme again popping up its head. Opposing this was the Corwen Bala & Porthmadog, via Trawsfynnydd and Ffestiniog, promoted by the powers of the G.W.R. along with a Bala & Dolgellau route. Consequently, the West Midland scheme was drastically reduced, and as a merger had by now been agreed upon, G.W.R. gave it full backing.

In the April of 1862 a Parliamentary Committee was set up to examine the schemes. It transpired that evidence given by the renowned engineer Benjamin Piercy to the Committee proved to be Thomas Savin's downfall.

The evidence revealed that if Savin received control of the Corwen to Barmouth line, he would then be suitably positioned to control a vast area to the point of routing traffic circuitously north via Rhyl rather than surrender it to the G.W.R., and despite the efforts of the formidable Edmund Denison as his legal counsel, Thomas Savin's proposed schemes were discarded.

The Corwen Bala & Porthmadog proposal was eventually reduced to a Corwen-Bala line and together with the Bala & Dolgellau, received Royal Assent on 30th June 1862. The companies of Thomas Savin received authorisation powers to run the Corwen to Dolgellau line but was disallowed control of the L.N.W.R link to Corwen.

This now paved the way clear for the completion of the line in favour of the Great Western. By the Act of 21st July 1863, the Bala & Dolgellau agreed with the Aberystwyth & Welsh Coast Railway on the junction and joint station at Dolgellau. During 1864 the Llangollen & Corwen and Corwen & Bala railways were continuing to purchase land and by the August of that year the station at Corwen was near to completion.

A section of the Corwen & Bala line (4¾ miles) from Corwen to Llandrillo with an intermediate station at Cynwyd was opened on 16th July 1866. By April 1st 1868 the remaining 7¾ miles of the Corwen & Bala railway was completed along with five small viaducts and a 76 yard long tunnel at Llandderfel. In addition there were also stations at Llandderfel and Bala.

1863

A comparatively quiet year, certainly by the lack of media coverage, with the exception of a standstill on the Berwyn Tunnel.

Berwyn Tunnel (work at a standstill)

For reasons unknown, work on the Berwyn Tunnel was at a standstill on the Corwen side, so reported the C & D H in its edition of 9th September 1863.

1864

The Great Western Railway Company were travelling through Corwen in June 1864, but it was more of a four-horse coach rather than the iron-horse, as the following advert appeared in the C & D H explained:-

Great Western Railway Travelling through North Wales, by the "Snowdon Tourist Four-Horse Coach".

From June 12th 1864 daily (not Sundays), leaving Llangollen Station on the arrival of trains from Leamington, Warwick, Birmingham, Wolverhampton, Hereford, Shrewsbury, Manchester,

Warrington, Liverpool and Chester and travelling through the Vale of Llangollen, Glyndyfrdwy, Corwen, by the Bridge and Waterfall of Pont-y-Glyn, Pentre Voelas, Betws-y-Coed and onwards to Caernarvon.

Proprietors:-

Edwards, Moltby, Jones, D. Williams, R. M. Williams & Moreton, Hand Hotel, Llangollen.

Progress on the Berwyn Tunnel

Progress on the Llangollen Corwen section continued almost unhindered, and in October 1864 the Baner reported that "only 30 yards of the Berwyn Tunnel remained to be completed". Some authors have incorrectly mentioned that the tunnel took only a little over 12 months to complete, but the Carnarvon & Denbigh Herald reported that work commenced on this in March 1862, and it is not surprising considering its 686 yards length and the difficulties experienced with the terrain that it took over two and a half years to complete.

1865

Llangollen and Corwen Railway

On Saturday January 14th the shrill whistle of a locomotive was first heard between Llangollen and Corwen, which was much more likely, in our opinion to "*call the spirits from the vasty deep*" than all the exploits of the mighty Glendower (*a reference to Owain Glyndwr*) as he swept along the beautiful valley of Glyndyfrdwy with his mailed warriors. A powerful engine and tender, with a first class carriage, brought H. Robertson Esq., M.P., Engineer of the G.W.R., Col. Tottenham, Chairman of the Llangollen and Corwen Branch, and a few of their friends along the line. Their safe arrival was greeted with the hurrahs of some hundreds of the inhabitants. After inspecting the new station &c. and partaking of a lunch at the

Owain Glyndwr Hotel, they took their departure well pleased it seemed at the progress of the works which are carried on under the able superintendence of A. Reid Esq., the indefatigable agent of the contractor. There is every probability that the pending day is not far distant.

Opening of the Llangollen to Corwen for Goods Traffic

The Carnarvon & Denbigh Herald in its edition of 21st January 1865 reported that on Thursday 19th inst., "*H. Robertson Esq., M.P., and his family left Crogen Hall (Llandrillo), his country seat, and went to London where he intends staying during the (Parliamentary) session.*

On his departure he gave orders that 20 tons of coal should be distributed among the poor in the parish of Llandrillo and the same amount in the parish of Llandderfel. It was his intention to have it distributed before leaving but there had been some draw-back on the Llangollen to Corwen line so that it could not be brought up. But we are glad to learn that the engine paid her first visit to Corwen on Saturday last the 14th, and it is expected that the coal will be up on one of the next days, and immediately afterwards the distribution of it will take place."

Black Diamond

Whatever the cause for the drawback there doesn't appear to be any report explaining this, but this had been rectified by the following month as the following report shows from the edition of the 24th February.

"On Wednesday 21st February 1865 at about 2 o'clock in the afternoon, many hundreds of inhabitants of Corwen had the pleasure of witnessing the arrival of the first goods train from Llangollen, consisting of an engine and tender and seven trucks of Broughton Coal ('black diamond' as it was called in the 'Baner'), the present of Henry Robertson Esq., M.P., to the poor of Llandrillo and Llandderfel. The following persons gave the gratuitous use of their teams to convey the coals to Llandrillo and Llandderfel (the liberal giver paying the road expenses) (WAGGONS) Mr Roberts, Tyfos; Mr J. H. Jones, Coedmolfa; Mr Thomas Jones, Brynmelyn; (CARTS) Rev. J. Wynne, Tyddyn Llan; Mr James Evans, Llechwedd; Mr Edward Ellis, Brynbwlan; Mr Ellis Thomas, Hafoty Ganol; Mr Thos. Bodden, Dolgadfa; Mrs Williams, Derwgoed."

Reduction in price of coal

One noteable and immediate effect of the opening of the railway for goods traffic was a reduction in the price of coal from 10d to 8d per hundredweight, this no doubt a result of cheaper transportation due to freight volume. (In 1860 the price was 1s 2d.)

Inspection and passing of line as satisfactory

The actual line from Llangollen to Corwen was inspected and passed by a Captain Rich as satisfactory for traffic and the commencement for such being on the 8th May 1865. (It was however on the 21st April that the line was officially opened when the first passengers made the first ever journey by train from Llangollen to Corwen). Despite this the line terminated at its junction with the Denbigh Ruthin & Corwen line, the station at this time not having being built. Eventually, by the 11th October 1865 the permanent station was opened. The station, built from designs by Mr Poultenay Smith of Shrewsbury, experienced a lengthy delay between the completion of the line and that of the station, the reason being the very severe winter of 1864/1865.

Official Opening of the Llangollen to Corwen Railway

The Carnarvon and Denbigh Herald reported in its issue of

Saturday 29th April 1865 on the official opening with the following heading:-

'Rejoicings in Honour of the Opening of the Llangollen and Corwen Railway' preceded by a report of the half-yearly meetings of three railway companies.

(Opening of the Llangollen to Corwen Railway - text from Carnarvon & Denbigh Herald, Record Office & Archives in Ruthin)

HALF YEARLY MEETINGS OF THE VALE OF LLANGOLLEN, LLANGOLLEN AND CORWEN, AND CORWEN AND BALA RAILWAY COMPANIES

On Saturday last the twelfth half-yearly meeting of the first, the tenth of the second, and the first of the third of the above companies were held at the Town Hall, Llangollen, pursuant to notice. There were present Colonel Tottenham, chairman, H. Robertson Esq., M.P., J. Robertson Esq., W. Wagstaff Esq., J. Jones Esq., Oswestry, Captain Reid, &c. Mr Richards, the secretary of the company, read the statement of accounts of the Vale of Llangollen Railway, from which it appeared that the receipts were £4,669. 17s. 1d., and the balance available for dividends. &c. £1,826. 4s. The reports stated "The directors have again the pleasure of reporting that the traffic during the past half-year exhibits a very satisfactory increase both in goods and passengers from the traffic of the corresponding half-year for 1863, and taking all the circumstances into consideration they feel themselves justified in recommending the payment of a dividend of three per cent. on the ordinary share capital, and of five per cent. on the preference share capital. It has been suggested that the expenditure in that portion of the Llangollen and Corwen Railway, which extends from the terminus of this railway to the points leading to the goods station, including the goods and passengers' station at Llangollen, should be treated as common and divided equally between the two companies, which arrangement the directors consider equitable, and recommend for adoption. The directors have every reason to expect that the railway to Corwen will be opened in the ensuing month. The directors retiring from office are Col. Tottenham, Capt. Reid. J.R. Ormsby Gore Esq., M.P., and the retiring auditor is W. Patchett Esq., all of whom are eligible for re-election.

The Chairman said - "In moving that the report just read be printed and circulated amongst the shareholders, it will be necessary for me to make a few remarks. The traffic as will be seen, is increasing very rapidly and steadily, not only up to the end of the half-year, but since the time when the accounts were made up. And, no doubt, when the Llangollen and Corwen line is opened, the receipts will increase even more rapidly. There will be a great amount of coal sent along, and lime and other things, which will be wanted at Corwen and neighbourhood. I shall not detain you any longer, but move that the report just read be adopted and printed and circulated among the proprietary".

The motion was seconded by Captain Reid, and carried unanimously.

The retiring directors and auditor were next unanimously re-elected, and this concluded the business of this company.

The Secretary then read the statement of accounts of the Llangollen and Corwen Railway, which showed the receipts to be £69,877, and the balance £1,008. 1s. 3d. The report stated:- "First,- the directors have the satisfaction of reporting that the line is now completed to Corwen, and only waits the inspection of the Officer of the Board of Trade to permit the line to be opened to the public. Second,- The past unusually severe winter has prevented the finishing of the station buildings, but they are rapidly being completed. Third,- It has been proposed to divide the cost of the portion of the line at Llangollen, including the passenger and goods stationed between the Vale of Llangollen Railway Company and this company, and the directors recommend that this proposal be carried out. Fourth,- Colonel Tottenham, J.R. Ormsby Gore, Esq., M.P., and Captain Reid, are the retiring directors, and offer themselves for re-election. Fifth,- The statement of receipts and expenditure is appended to the report as in the case of the other company".

The Chairman said - "I beg to propose that the report which has just been read be adopted and printed for circulation among the shareholders. It is well known that we had a preliminary opening yesterday. The line was found in excellent order, and a large party went down and seemed to enjoy the scenery and the good things which were provided for them at Corwen (hear, hear). The line, as stated, is finished, and we are only waiting for the arrival of the inspector to open it for the public. When that is done, there is no doubt that the beauty of the scenery will attract great numbers this and succeeding seasons, and that the results will be very satisfactory to the shareholders" (hear, hear).

Mr J. Robertson begged to second the motion which, with the election of the retiring directors and auditors subsequently moved, received unanimous assent.

Mr Jones begged to read the report of the directors of the Corwen and Bala Railway Company, which was as follows:- "Your directors have to report that they have been occupied during the past half-year in acquiring the land for the railway. They have also to report a considerable progress in the works along the line, and the completion of about a mile of the railway at the junction with the Llangollen and Corwen, and Denbigh, Ruthin and Corwen Railway, and which is at this moment waiting the inspection of the Board of Trade. The director retiring on this occasion is C.W. Wynn, Esq., M.P., who offers himself for re-election.

The Chairman said - "I beg to move that the report which has just been read be adopted, printed, and circulated among the shareholders. There is very little for me to make any remarks upon. The report explains everything as far it is necessary; but we hope that the progress of the railway will continue under the able conduct of our engineer and contractors. Of course, it is impossible to state any particular time when the line will be finished, but I have no doubt it will be pushed forward with vigour. It will be a great addition to our traffic when the line is opened through in connection with the Dolgelley and Bala Railway, the contract for which has been taken" (hear, hear). The motion was seconded by Mr Robertson, Mr Wynn was re-elected, Mr Wagstaff was also elected on the directory, and Mr John Evans was re-elected auditor, which concluded the business of the day, and the best thanks of the meeting were passed to the Chairman.

The Chairman did not think he was deserving of any thanks for the little which had been done that day; still it could not but be gratifying to find that the shareholders in all of the three companies had shown their continued confidence in the directors by not thinking it necessary to attend these meetings in any number.

The proceedings then terminated.

Rejoicings in Honour of the Opening of the Llangollen and Corwen Railway

This beautiful line of railway was opened, in a preliminary manner, with great rejoicings on the 21st inst. Amongst all the beauties of the Principality, the Vale of Llangollen holds a prominent place, and perhaps that portion of it stretching from the town of Llangollen to that of Corwen is the most striking. The day of the formal opening was superb, the sun shone brightly, and the sky was without a cloud. A special excursion train left Llangollen about noon, filled with a large and fashionable company of friends and well-wishers of the line. Leaving the temporary station of the Vale of Llangollen Railway the train proceeded to the new joint station of the two railways, passing under Llangollen bridge, which, at one time, was considered one of the wonders of Wales. The toll collector's house having been removed, a new one has been built by the company of cut-stone in the castellated style as a "tète du pont". This, as well as the several stations on this line we are upon, is built from designs by Mr Poultenay Smith of Shrewsbury. In consequence of the unusually severe winter some of the stations have not been completed; but they are all of a very chaste and appropriate character, and very far superior in architectural design to that of railway stations generally.

Having picked up some carriages which had brought down a party of visitors from Corwen, the train proceeded amidst the ringing cheers of throngs of the inhabitants assembled in the neighbourhood, passing on the right the goods station, which has now been open for some little time, and which showed unmistakeable evidence of large traffic. The train soon crossed the Dee by a very substantially built, but light looking bridge, adjoining the works of the Llangollen Slab and Slate Company on the north side of the river. In a moment after, on leaving these behind, we found ourselves in the opening of the charming little valley in which is situate that magnificent monument of the olden time, the ruins of Valle Crucis Abbey, a passing glimpse of which interesting ruins we obtain, the pointed gables seeming to spring up into the clear atmosphere, and contrasting sharply with the graceful grouping of majestic mountains with which Valle Crucis is surrounded on either side. Then we arrived at Berwyn station. Close beneath is the old Chain Suspension Bridge, which some clever Cymro long years ago, finding the distance of passing around over the bridge at Llangollen to be highly inconvenient, decided on executing, and from this structure it is stated - from little events great causes have again and again resulted - Telford took the design for the Menai Suspension Bridge. That great engineer in his passing up and down "the great Holyhead road", as it was called years ago, cast his eyes upon this little bridge, and then the spark communicated itself to his fertile mind, and the great conception was formed which resulted in that magnificent and wonderful achievement spanning the Menai Straits, which is, so to speak, light and graceful in appearance as a gossamer's web, but which is in itself a monument of the power of English intellect and the majesty of England's greatness. But we must recur to the events of the day; and moving away from the Berwyn Station, a little further on another of Telford's works comes in view, namely the weir at the head of the feeder of the Ellesmere Canal. We cannot resist the claim of this weir to notice, not only for the engineering ability with which the work is constructed, but we must for a moment draw attention to its elegant formation in the shape of a crescent, and the beautiful proportions of the work itself. As the bright waters of the Dee dash over the weir they seem to wear a grand fringe of sparkling silver spray. On the opposite side of the river are seen Bryntysilio, the residence of Mrs Lynes, and Llantysilio Hall, that of Captain Reid. Between these mansions is the quaint Church of Llantysilio, the parish church formerly served by the monks of Valle Crucis. The church yard contains some venerable yew trees. Proceeding on our journey, next there comes in view - above the weir and the broad green meadows circling down thereto - the beautiful mansion of Plas Berwyn, the summer residence of Colonel Tottenham, which stands on a gentle eminence like a fairy palace of peace and rest in the midst of the grandly wild and multitudinous mountains by which it is surrounded. This house is beautifully situated in the midst of woods and extensive plantations. The ornamental grounds are laid out with much taste and beauty of design, and a full view of them is obtained from the line by the kindness of Colonel Tottenham, who is the chairman of this and the two railways in connection with it. But the respected owner we rejoice to say, since becoming possessor of Plas Berwyn estate, a good many years ago, has identified himself with the locality unmistakeably, - has become a Welshman in spirit and in heart, and has brought all his great ability into effect, and rendered every assistance in his power to promote not only the progress and efficiency of the railway communication in the country, but the well-being and happiness of the town of Llangollen and neighbourhood. The line runs for five miles through Col. Tottenham's estate. At Plas Berwyn a salute was fired from some small cannon, which was responded to with rounds of cheering. The train then entered the Berwyn Tunnel. It is 700 yards long, and such was the hardness of the rock, that it took more than two and a half years of constant work, night and day, to cut through it. On emerging from the tunnel on the other side of the Bwlch, we found ourselves carried into the court, so to speak, of the great Welsh chieftain Owen Glyndwr. The line passes through the portion of the Vale of Llangollen, which is known as "Glyn Dyfrdwy" (the vale of two rivers). But close by the line, where it leaves the tunnel, the wizard Dee spreads itself in all its beauty before us, and there were three islets smiling in the sun, expanding their flowers and their foliage as if to welcome us again into the bright scenes of light and verdure. The line follows for the remainder of the distance the banks of the Dee, which is alternately dark pool and foaming rapid, the hills on each side rising abruptly and to a considerable height, clothed with wood and plantation, with dark mountains in the distance covered with heather. About half-way the train passes Glyndyfrdwy Station, near which a bridge is about being built across the Dee. About half a mile further on is Berwyn Inn, a favourite resort of anglers, as it is in the middle of the celebrated Glyndwr Fishery Preserve. We next passed under "Owen Glyndwr's Mount". Here it was, according to "ye ancient chronicle", that the chieftain lived: here it was he marshalled his legions, and here it was that he fought for those rights ultimately recognised and accorded by the English, and which have been guaranteed for so long under that constitution which renders the sovereign of this great nation as dear to the people of Wales as to those of her own capital.

Aye, we may say we are one people, and the happiness and prosperity of England is the happiness and prosperity of every part of the empire, Wales included. But centuries ago - the Kymric mind still loves to dwell upon the story - Owen Glyndwr, from his eyrie on this mound of observation received tidings from Castle Dinas

Glyndyfrdwy Station from the Llangollen end. The Station House is on the left, the signal-box on the right. Photo: Lens of Sutton

Carrog Station with a Manor-Class arriving from Corwen. Photo: Lens of Sutton

Bran that the foe was approaching. His great soul was moved, and from his lips issued the martial cry "Arm, arm! the enemy is at hand!" It required but a small exercise of imagination on our part to fancy that today the same mighty spirit might re-visit the scene to his earthly life so dear, and that a fervent joy would fill his soul when he saw the harbinger of trade and modern civilization, the messenger of peace, and the builder of a nation's prosperity rushing up and passing by in triumph his entrenched position - hurrying on with gladsome welcome to his beloved old town of Corwen.

The train soon arrived at Llansantffraid (or Carrog) station, where, as at other parts of the line, many persons were assembled to salute the excursionists with ringing cheers. After passing this station we see Rhaggatt on the right, the beautiful residence of J. Lloyd, Esq., on the left the great Holyhead road comes abreast with the rail and the river, and soon after we arrived at Corwen, where large numbers of persons were assembled, who welcomed heartily the arrival of the preliminary opening train. The line we should state is eleven miles long, and will be opened probably early in the ensuing month, as it is only waiting for the satisfaction of the government inspector to be opened for traffic. The engineer was that indefatigable pioneer of railways, Henry Robertson Esq., M.P., and Messrs Brassey and Field, the contractors.

THE FESTIVE DEMONSTRATIONS AT CORWEN

It is not a little curious that the inhabitants of this noted beautiful little town are persuaded that within the last few months the sun has, by "some degrees", improved his position towards them! There is more sunshine, more life and more warmth than used to be in the olden time. Must we attribute this to the advent of the railway? We must suppose that these genial feelings find their origin in the spirit which has been infused into the good people of the town, and which was so joyously manifested on this occasion.

The town was gaily decorated with flags and banners, and a triumphal arch spanned the roadway coming up from the station. The fine band of the Ruthin volunteers was engaged for the festivity, and added their enlivening strains to the general hilarity of the day.

THE OPENING BANQUET

Soon after the arrival of the train the gentlemen connected with the railway and their guests repaired to luncheon in a handsomely decorated pavilion, erected close to the Owen Glyndwr Arms, on the site where it is hoped that the new market hall of Corwen will stand. The interior of the tent was tastefully adorned with mottoes, evergreens, choice exotics &c.

The door was boarded with planks, and the tables were laid with great elegance. The general arrangements, and the very handsome collation - which was graced by the presence of the ladies - were much praised, the prevailing sentiment being one of solid satisfaction, which must have been very gratifying to the host and hostess, Mr and Mrs Moltby, who have so long and ably carried on the business at the famed Owen Glyndwr Arms Hotel.

Colonel Tottenham presided supported in the vice-chairs by Mr Robertson, M.P., and Mr Wagstaff and the list of guests invited included:- Colonel Myddleton Biddulph, M.P.; Sir Watkin Williams Wynn, Bart., M.P.; Mr Townshend Mainwaring, M.P.; the Honourable Mrs Tottenham and the Misses Tottenham, Plas Berwyn; the Hon. Major Fitzmaurice and Miss Fitzmaurice; Mr C.W. Tottenham; Dr and the Misses Robertson; Mr Morris Roberts; Capt. Reid; Mr Price, Llanrhaiadr; Mr J.O. Binger; L. and N.W., Chester; Mr Martin Smith, V.C.R.; and the gentlemen connected with the Denbigh, Ruthin and Corwen Raiway, Mr Hugh Jones; Mr R. Baker; Mr G. Dickin; Mr Reid; Mr Cruickshank; Lady Marshall; Mr H. Jones, Maesmawr; Mr Lynes, Bryntysilio; Mr Mourier,

Woodlands; Miss Williams, ditto; Mr D. Hughes, Minffordd; Captain Sewell, R.N.; Rev. John Wynne, Llandrillo; Mr Marcus Louis, Ruthin; Rev. Thomas Kirk, ditto; Mr James Walker; Mr Jones, Oswestry; Mr Clement, Shrewsbury; Mr Thomas Davies, Royal Hotel, Llangollen; Mr and Miss Edwards, Hand Hotel, Llangollen; Mr T. Helps, Chester; Rev. H.T. Edwards, Llangollen; Mr Stephens, Chester; Rev. D. Jones, Llangollen; Mr J.C. Edwards, Trefnant; Mr Brandt, C.E.; Mr E. Parry; Mr C. Richards; secretary of the railway and party; Rev. Mr Williams, Llangor (*should this read Llangar?*); Mr C. Mackintosh; Mr J. Grant; Mr D. Brookes; Mr D. Pritchard; Mr R. White; Mr Price Jones; Mr R.J. Venables; Mr W. Foulkes; Mr N. Jones; Rev. E.J. Owen and Mrs Owen, Llanfair, Ruthin; Rev. John Jones; Mr and Miss Jones, Llangwm; &c, &c.

Grace being said and the repast concluded.

The Chairman proposed in succession the usual loyal episcopal and patriotic toasts which were responded in the noblest manner, the band playing appropriate airs.

The Vice-chairman Mr Robertson, M.P., in proposing the next toast said it was one which he was sure they would all agree with him, was the toast of the day - "Success to the Llangollen and Corwen Railway, and the health of the chairman, Col. Tottenham" (cheers). It was clear from the way in which the simple announcement of the toast was received, that it required no speech, but he believed it would not be considered respectful if he were so very brief and laconic. He felt sure, by what he had seen that day, that the toast of prosperity to the Llangollen and Corwen Railway was one in which they would all agree most heartily. It was in itself but a very small railway, only about ten miles long, but it had its peculiarities that were not uninteresting to railway men. Many experienced railway men had travelled over it, and they said it was a very interesting ten miles of railway (applause). They had some difficulty in escaping out of Llangollen, but they endeavoured to do so without interfering much with the old town, and he thought they had done it without detracting from the beauties of the place (hear, hear). They passed along the valley, through the narrow gorge, and came to the crossing of the Dee, and then they had some difficulty in getting a bridge founded on the bottom of the river. They had to contend with the loose rocks in the bottom of the Dee, but they did it successfully (applause). They had a capital water dog in the agent, Mr Reid, and a better piece of work was never done than that bridge on the boulders of the Dee. It was done well, and there it was to speak for itself. Then the line came to the turnpike road, the bridge, the canal, and the public road on the other side, and so they passed on to the Berwyn to as pretty a spot as any railway could pass through. He was one of those who thought a railway should enjoy the pretty places as well as other means of communication. Then they came to their greatest difficulty, and that was no trifle. They had the Berwyn to pass through, and owing to the height of the ground above, they could only work at two points. Besides, they had to work at a sharp curve, and on an incline, but with the assistance of the engineers and Mr Reid, they made a good job of it, though he was sorry to say it occupied a long time, and human nature could not do it faster. For two years and eight months they were working at it day and night incessantly, for twenty four hours. However, they got through the darkness, and then there was nothing but the pleasant meandering journey along the Dee to Corwen, and he hoped their difficulties were now over, and that the pleasant trip they had had that day, limited only because the tent was limited, would soon be followed by the opening of the line to all, and that others besides themselves would enjoy that excursion (applause). But they must not look upon that line as merely ten miles of railway. It was part of an important system for North Wales - a most important route right through the heart of the country, and he was glad to tell them that arrangements were, he would say, perfected by which the extension of the line to Dolgelley would be completed (applause). That was but one part of the route, for this railway would also form the inlet towards that from Bala to Festiniog, and the west coast of Carnarvonshire (applause).

Then they must not forget the Vale of Clwyd, and the arrangements with that line. He looked at this railway from Llangollen as being of great national advantage in developing the resources of North Wales in a way most effective for the industry of the country (hear, hear). Before such a company as that he would not speak of the benefits of railway communication. In Wales they wanted the manufacturers of England, and other articles, and England wanted various things in return. Hitherto Wales had been to a great extent shut up, but the development of her resources and her industry by the introduction of railway communication would tend to improve all classes. It would add to the wealth and the employment of the country, and raise all to a higher level than they now enjoyed (applause). He was sure that in that result those who promoted the railways would find their greatest reward, as well as obtaining that other reward, which, they ought to obtain as proprietors, from the profits of the traffic (applause).

Whilst they looked at the benefits which the country would obtain from the introduction of the railways, they would not forget those to whom they were indebted for it, and first of those who had steadfastly promoted railways let him name Colonel Tottenham (applause). When they were getting the line to Llangollen, he was there to assist them, and they got that line, and they had made his own Corwen line - for they might call it his own, since half of the line went through the gallant colonel's property, and he (Mr Robertson) hoped they would continue to have the benefit of his untiring industry and assistance in the lines to Bala and Dolgelley and the other extensions in North Wales (applause). He (Mr Robertson) would no longer trespass on their time, but ask them to drink success to the Llangollen and Corwen railway and the health of the chairman (applause).

The Chairman said, on behalf of the directors of the Llangollen and Corwen Railway Company he begged to thank them most heartily. Mr Robertson had so ably described the difficulties of the line in engineering and other points of view, and also the advantages that would result from railway communication, that it was unnecessary for him to travel over the same track. For himself he had only to say that when he found his lot partly cast in that beautiful valley, he of course wished to do everything he could to improve its condition, and there was no way in which, it was evident to him, he could so effectually do it as by promoting the introduction of railways (hear, hear). He fortunately met with Mr Robertson several years ago, and they had worked together - at least he (the chairman) might say he had been a humble assistant of Mr Robertson's in carrying out the second stage of that system of railways. Whenever he (the chairman) undertook anything he always did it with a will. Perhaps he did not always go so far as he ought to do, but it was not his own fault he did not. Before he sat down he must beg that they would allow him to propose a toast - the health of the gentleman who really was the prime mover in that railway system. The directors had comparatively easy work to do. For himself, he had watched the progress of the works for the last two years and a half, and he might also claim to be an assistant of their friend, Mr Reid's, for he was on the line almost as much as that gentleman was himself (laughter).

But the prime mover was their worthy engineer (applause). To his energy and perseverance they were indebted not only for the Vale of Llangollen line and that railway, but for the prospect of further extensions (hear, hear). He had some very up-hill work in more senses of the word than one, in making his way through that valley up to Corwen. It was unnecessary to detain them any longer, and he (the chairman) would propose the health of Mr Robertson, M.P. for Shrewsbury and their engineer (applause).

Mr Robertson begged to thank them most sincerely for the honour they had done him. He had enjoyed the good fortune of carrying out other lines of railway in Wales, both north and south. It was now some twenty years since he had the satisfaction of commencing the first railway south of Chester, and of carrying it through Shrewsbury, a town for which he had the greatest respect and from which he hailed, and one to which he ought to pay all respect (laughter). He helped to carry on the line to Hereford and South Wales, and was proud of having been the means, with others, of placing in a perfect and finished state that railway by which both the Great Western and North Western competed for the traffic of North and South Wales (applause). But when executing these lines, if tired and jaded with the work, there was one valley to which he liked to turn, and there with rod and coracle to enjoy and refresh himself (applause). And when the fish would not nibble, it was his amusement to think where he would place the railway which he had determined to carry out; and he was exceedingly proud that day to find his hopes and purposes so fully realised, and to have that pleasant excursion with many friends along the banks of the Dee (applause). It was but an instalment of what, with the assistance of those interested in the locality, they hoped to do in the way of railway communcation, and he should be exceedingly proud to see the day when that railway would be further extended through the Principality (applause). They could not forget those whose out with them on the accomplishment of this work (*the sentence, despite its syntactical error, is as it was written in the C & DH*). He could not forget his poor brother, Charley Dean. If he had been spared he would greatly have enjoyed being present with them that day. He had left a pleasant memory, and he (Mr Robertson) should always see him in those works (applause). Those who were left would do what they could for the benefit of the locality. He was interested, as a resident, a Merionethshire proprietor - not a very large one, but still large enough to give him an interest in the country, and he should be delighted to help, with others, in carrying out railway communication in the Principality (hear, hear). He could not sit down without calling attention to the man who above all others, had been mainly instrumental in carrying out the work - Mr Brassey and his partner, Mr Field (applause). Great as was the engineering profession, and the work of the men who practically carried out what they designed, among them no man stood so high as his (Mr Robertson's) friend, Mr Brassey (applause). More than twenty years ago, when he (Mr Robertson) was a young railway engineer, and could find no one to carry out the Shrewsbury and Chester line for the estimate, he met with Mr Brasey in a railway carriage, and showed him the estimate. Mr Brassey said "Young man, you have plenty of money and I will do it for the estimate" (hear, hear). Mr Brassey carried out the line successfully, as he deserved to do, from his energy and worthiness in every respect.

The same gentleman enabled him (Mr Robertson) to carry out the Llangollen and Corwen line. He (Mr Brassey) was a large proprietor in those lines, and plainly showed, by what he did, that he believed they were worth making (applause). Those lines were carried out as well as men and materials could carry them out, and in a most appropriate manner. No money was foolishly wasted in fine work, but the work was substantial and would bear comparison with any, and it would remain when both Mr Brassey and he were gone as a monument of what such work ought to be (applause). He (Mr Robertson) asked them to drink a bumper to the health of Messrs Brassey and Field (applause).

Mr Field, in responding, said he naturally felt very proud at so often being called upon to represent so great a man as Mr Brassey, for his numerous engagements prevented him from being present on such occasions as that. His absence was always a great disappointment, and in the present instance particularly so, since, as Mr Robertson had told them, and he (Mr Field) could bear witness to the fact, it was chiefly owing to the liberal and enterprising spirit of Mr Brassey that they were able to come there that day to enjoy the hospitality of their excellent friend Mr Robertson (applause). The advantages of railway communication generally, and the many great benefits which that line was calculated to bestow on the immediate neighbourhood, had been so ably set forth by the worthy chairman and Mr Robertson, that it only remained for him (Mr Field) to express his most sincere hope that those advantages might be most fully realised and that the railway might prove both advantageous to the locality through which it passed and remunerative to those who were its promoters, and had invested their capital in it (applause).

Victorian environmentalist's?

Sometimes, in beautiful places, they heard people exclaiming "What a shame the railway should be brought here to spoil the scenery!" It was true they had come through some very beautiful scenery that day, but he could not imagine anyone so deficient in taste as to think that the train, with its freight of beauty and loveliness, did any other than add enchantment to the view (laughter and applause). He was glad to say that their worthy chairman was so satisfied that the railway was an addition to the scene, that he insisted upon having an invisible fence placed along the line on his estate, that he might enjoy the prospect of the trains (applause). He (Mr Field) was glad to have this opportunity of thanking the gallant colonel for the kind manner in which he had rendered every assistance and given every facility to the contractors in the construction of the line, and that he (Mr Field) most sincerely hoped that his (the gallant colonel's) most sanguine anticipations of benefit from the great exertions which he had used in bringing about the railway, would be most fully realised (applause).

The Chairman wished fully to endorse everything Mr Robertson had said respecting Messrs Brassey and Field, and at the same time to bear witness to the excellent conduct, generally speaking, of all the men engaged on the line (hear, hear). They had been engaged for two winters through about five miles of his property, where he had a few pheasants, and he was not aware that he had lost one of them (hear, hear).

Mr Robertson asked them to drink the health of a most excellent man, "Mr Reid" (applause). There was no one to whom they owed more for the practical carrying out of the works, and he did his duty towards all engineers, contractors, owners of property, and shareholders (applause). Mr Reid said he thanked them all most sincerely. He could make railways, but he coud not make speeches (applause).

Mr Wagstaff said he had permission to propose a toast which he was sure would meet with a warm reception. It was the health of the "Visitors" - the ladies and gentlemen who had honoured them with their presence that day. He would couple with the toast the name of Major Fitzmaurice (applause).

Major Fitzmaurice returned thanks in a humorous speech.

Mr Charles W. Tottenham, coxswain of the University Eight, in proposing "the Ladies", said the Vale of Llangollen ought to be proud of the fair representatives sent to Corwen that day (applause). He believed the original Jenny Jones of Llangollen was not present, but he was sure there were many others there who might with equal justice have been celebrated in immortal verse (laughter and applause).

Captain Reid responded on behalf of the ladies.

The Chairman gave "the health of Mrs Robertson" (applause).

Mr Robertson said he begged most heartily to return thanks on behalf of Mrs Robertson.

Major Fitzmaurice gave "the health of the Navvies of the United Kingdom", and spoke in high terms of their general character and conduct as compared with those of similar classes in other countries where he had travelled (applause). He asked the company to drink it with all the honour due to labour and integrity (applause). Mr Reid humourously responded saying he was a "navvy" and was proud of his calling (cheers).

The proceedings concluded with a "*cheer for Cymru*", proposed by Mr Robertson.

The special train shortly afterwards left for Llangollen, and very soon rural sports were improvised, which created great merriment, the climbing of a greased pole for prizes of a leg of mutton, a new hat, &c., adding its laughter moving causes to the general fun which was wound up after nightfall with a grand display of fireworks.

1866

Coach

A four-horse coach service operated from Corwen to Bala every morning. This would meet the train on arrival at 10:25 and return from Bala at 2 p.m. to meet the 4 p.m. train at Corwen.

As the number of railway passengers increased it was inevitable that insurance would eventually find its corner as the following report shows.

Railway Insurance

The Railway Passengers' Assurance Company, in their advertisement, claim that £250,000 had been paid as compensation for accidents of all kinds. For an annual premium of 3 shillings to 6 shillings and 5 d (15 p to 32 p) security of 1000 shillings in case of death and 6 shillings per week "while laid up by injury".

This advertisement in the Carnarvonshire and Denbighshire

Herald in the May displays how the railway was slowly beginning to make travel accessible to the masses:-

Gwyliau y Sulgwyn

A special and cheap train from various locations including Corwen to Birkenhead.

Fare: 4 shillings return.

The advertisement also stated that a number of ministers from both South and North Wales would be on the excursion - did the fact that it stated that ministers would be making this journey influence the type and number of persons who booked on this excursion? I'm sure it did as religion was a dominant feature of peoples' lives in that period.

The Iron Horse visits Llandrillo

This report in the C&DH: "The line called Corwen and Bala Railway is carried on with great vigour. The branch from Corwen to Llandrillo is nearly, if not fully completed. The 'Iron Horse' has visited Llandrillo station several times and the other day brought with him with great ease about 60 tons of materials.

The line is to be inspected in the course of a week, and if passed, will be open a few days later. Between Llandrillo and Bala there are some heavy works and cuttings which probably will take another 12 months to complete".

4-Horse Coach Excursion

By June 1866 the railway was increasing the number of tourist's using the train and advertisements began to appear for coach and horse excursions to parts of North Wales not yet accessible by train, as this advert in the C&DH details:-

'The Snowdon Tourist 4-horse coaches meeting trains on arrival at Corwen from Manchester, Warrington, Liverpool,

Chester, Wolverhampton, Birmingham, Ludlow, Shrewsbury, travelling to the foot of Snowdon, arriving back at Corwen in time for all departing trains'.

Proprietors: Moltby, Jones, Price, Williams & Moreton, Owain Glyndwr Hotel, Corwen.

The following advertisement highlighted the travelling available to people in the Vale of Clwyd joining up with the GWR at Corwen.

Picnic or Pleasure Parties

As from July 2nd to October 31st, 1st, 2nd and 3rd Class return tickets at Single Fare for the double journey will be issued at all stations on the Denbigh, Ruthin & Corwen railway to parties of not less than 6 x 1st class or 10 x 2nd/3rd Class

Passengers desirous of making 'Pleasure Excursions' to places on or adjacent to this railway, the Vale of Clwyd or Llangollen & Corwen Railways; also to Chirk, Ruabon, Wrexham, Gresford, Chester and Shrewsbury and the principal stations on the G.W.R.

In the November a case at the County Court in Corwen against the G.W.R. for the loss of a dog:-

County Court at Corwen before A.J. Jones Esq. Judge.

A Thomas Ellis brought a case against the G.W.R. for the value of a pointer dog which was sent from Caernarvon to Corwen. The dog, fastened by a chain was delivered to a porter in Corwen to be sent to Bala to the plaintiff but was lost.

His honour found for the plaintiff with 11 shillings damages and costs.

1867

The following report in November in the C&DH reports on the employment boost for the area but at the same time highlights the problem regarding temporary lodging for the navvies.

Corwen, Bala and Dolgelley Railways

We are now informed that there is plenty of work on the Corwen - Bala line for railway labourers but strange to say that no accommodation can be found. The foreman of the works tells us on application of employment being made, is reported to have said "Yes we can find you work for the next six months, but you must find your own lodging accommodation. The result of which is none to be found is that the poor tramping navvies have to give the work up."

Why don't the railways build wooden huts and let them out to the men to their advantage, for the length of the navvies' employment? Or if they don't wish to do this, why not allow some of the enterprising tradespeople of Corwen to provide the necessary accommodation, and arrange moderate rents by the occupants.

It would be an immense comfort to the poor fellows who have returned homewards, one and all saying he could not find a place to lie down in. There need be no fear on the score of non-payment of rent, as it could easily be guaranteed by the workmen agreeing with the keeper of the pay sheets for the rent of their habitations to be regularly deducted. It is hoped that some persons of influence will take up this distressing case which to the poor appears not unlike the punishment of 'TANTALUS'.

In some areas the railway companies did allow the navvies to build shelters, but these provided only shelter with cramped sleeping arrangements and were extremely harsh conditions to live in.

This report of a railway company employee on a charge of larcency appeared in the C&DH edition of December 7th 1867:

Larcency by a railway porter

Alfred Allen, employed at Llandrillo Rail Station, was brought up in custody of P.C. Evans on a charge of having stolen a double-barrelled gun, the property of his employers, the Great Western Railway Company, as bailees.

The offence was indirectly proved by Mr Roberts, Station Master, Llandrillo, and Peter Hughes, who bought the gun from the prisoner, who alleged that he bought it from a stranger at the station. Committed for trial at the next Quarter Sessions at Bala, bail being allowed, but not given. The prisoner has a wife and children living at Llandrillo. Inspector Perret conducted the case for the prosecution and Mr Owen David Hughes defended.

Their worships sat from 11 a.m. till 7 p.m. which is rather an unusual thing for them to do.

In the December this report details the first train journey to Bala:-

Corwen & Bala Railway

It is evident now that this line is drawing nigh its completion. The permanent road has been laid down all the way from Llandrillo to Bala, and all materials for the work conveyed along the line, so that the remainder of it can be carried on more vigourously. The Bala people will have the pleasure of witnessing the odd "Iron Horse" paying its first journey to Bala Station on Tuesday the 31st inst., as it is the intention of H. Robertson Esquire, Crogen Hall, to convey the Magistrates of Corwen District on an engine from Llandrillo to Bala, thus giving the privelege and the pleasure of travelling by railway for the first time to Bala Quarter Session. It is not known yet when the line will be opened for public traffic, but it is the intention of the company to do so as soon as possible, probably in a month or six weeks.

1868

Another section of the Llangollen & Corwen Railway opened on the 1st April 1868 and the following report highlights how important a part the railway was to the people of the area bringing a whole new world of social and economic benefits:-

Celebration of the opening of the Bala Railway.

The public opening for goods and passenger traffic of the Llangollen & Corwen Railway to Bala took place on the 1st of April. The line distance from Corwen to Bala is 12 miles and is single track all the way.

Steepest gradient is one in 150.

Corwen station was thronged with excursionist's at 10.30 a.m. awaiting the special train to convey them to Bala.

'Banquet' at the White Lion and Royal Hotel for the dignitaries, but a subscription was raised in the town to treat the workmen on the line at the Carrier's Arms Inn.

By the June the Denbigh, Corwen and Bala Railway Companies were facing financial difficulties as the following report of the half-yearly meeting of the companies reveals:-

Half-yearly meeting of the Denbigh, Corwen and Bala Railway Companies

Half-yearly meeting of the Denbigh, Corwen and Bala Railway Companies held on 28th May reported that revenue from all sources amounted to 5500/-, an increase of 650/- over the same period of 1866. This was due mainly to an increase in passenger traffic now that the line was open through to Bala. Lack of shed accommodation led to exposure from weather causing damage to some carriages, but the permanent way was in good order excepting some sleepers which have to be replaced due to decay.

The company was at this time facing financial difficulties and a receiver of the earnings of the line had been appointed by the Court of Chancery.

The directors would endeavour in the next half-year to prepare a scheme of arrangement under the Companies Act 1867 by which the present proceedings in the Court of Chancery may be terminated, and this they feel to be the only course of action to place the company on a sound footing.

Despite the difficulties encountered by the railway companies, the railway continued to bring further economic advantages to the area as this report shows in the July:-

Cheap day excursion

The opening of the line through to Bala had created another 'cheap-day excursion to Bala Lake', a 1 hour 50 minute journey from Denbigh at 7s 6d return fare 1st Class, 2s 9d other classes (fares for double journey on Tuesdays and Fridays).

In October it was reported that the journey time from Corwen to London varied from between 7 hours 40 minutes to 9 hours. No reason is given for this inconsistency but it could well be due to lengthier stoppages on some journeys.

1869

The railways have always imposed heavy fines for all infringements of their by-laws, but the following report in January 1869 of one case appears to be a very harsh judgement - forty shillings (£2) must have been a fortune!

Offenders against the Railway By-Laws

A Henry Parry was charged on the information of Mr Buckton, Station Master at Corwen, with having travelled from Llangollen to Corwen without taking a ticket with the intention of defrauding the Company. As this was not the first offence, the full penalty of 40 shillings (£2) and costs was inflicted.

Corwen to London in 6 hours and 40 minutes

By the February the journey time to London from Corwen had been reduced, this varying from 6 hours 40 minutes to 8 hours 55 minutes. This shows a remarkable decrease of one hour for the minimum time in only 3 months.

Corwen Slate Quarry

The railway was beginning to show its commercial potential in the local economy as the C&DH reported in June that there was "a thriving industry at Penarth Quarry, 2½ miles from Corwen Station on the Llangollen & Corwen Railway".

Adjoining Corwen and Llangollen turnpike road via a new road through Carrog Afon farm and will be connected with a tramway which is in the course of formation on the incline.

Vast quantities of slate are quarried it reported, employing between 80 and 90 persons, and that the agents of the quarry

Cynwyd Station approach from Corwen end. Photo: Lens of Sutton

Llandrillo Station. Photo: OPC/BR collection

recommend the employment of additional hands to supply the orders.

Due to the railway's location there had been an increase in production which had been estimated at 500 tons for the last three months, and could be delivered to various parts of England for 7 s 6 d (37 ½ p) per ton.

1870

In October, a letter to the C&DH - "desiring to call attention of its readers who may find themselves unfortunate victims should their luggage be, by accident, mislabelled to a station otherwise than their destination, and on application for it upon arrival, the railway officials will not only delay forwarding it, but charge the unfortunate victim for such detention of the luggage.

The correspondent also claims that if you are in danger of losing a train and therefore too late to purchase a ticket for the said journey, the order of the railway company is to the effect that when the passenger arrives at his/her destination he is subjected to some fearful interrogation.

Time-Tables

The report in February 1869 that the journey time from Corwen to London had been reduced to 6 hours 40 mins minimum is brought into question with the following time-table on page 101. This clearly shows the minimum journey time between Corwen and London to be 7 hours 45 minutes which is 1 hour 5 minutes longer and 5 minutes longer than what was reported to be the journey time back in October 1868.

Time-Table of the Llangollen & Corwen Railway

Dolgelley to London - October 1870

	a.m.	a.m.	a.m.	p.m.	p.m	p.m.
DOLGELLEY	-	8.30	10.30		4.00	6.35
Bontnewydd	-	8.50	10.39		4.09	6.44
Drws-y-Nant	-	8.52	10.51		4.21	6.56
Llanuwchllyn	-	9.05	11.05		4.35	7.10
BALA	-	9.17	11.15		4.47	7.23
Llandderfel	-	9.27	11.25		4.56	7.33
Llandrillo	-	9.35	11.32		5.03	7.40
Cynwyd	-	9.45	11.40		5.10	7.50
CORWEN	8.05	9.55	11.55	2.30	5.20	8.00
Carrog	8.12	10.02	12.02	2.37	5.30	
Glyndyfrdwy	8.20	10.10	12.07	2.44	5.38	
LLANGOLLEN		8.37	10.23	12.22	3.04	5.55
RUABON	9.00	10.46	12.45	3.27	6.18	
Wolverhampton		11.44	2.28	-	5.35	9.30
Birmingham	12.07	3.00	-	6.11	10.10	
LONDON	3.50	6.50	-	10.40		
Journey-time	7.45	8.55		8.10		

1871

Another accident was reported on the 8th of July in the C&DH but on this occasion there were no human casualties.

Railway Accident

A collision occurred on Tuesday morning last, near Corwen railway station, but, fortunately, unattended with injury or loss of life. A goods train was on its way from Ruabon for Dolgelley, and when against Corwen station, it came into collision with a shunting engine which was proceeding in an opposite direction. The rails were very slippery owing to the heavy rains, and the drivers and stokers of the engines, seeing that a collision was inevitable and being unable to stop their respective engines, jumped from their locomotives to the ground, and escaped uninjured. The engines were damaged.

One of the main engineers of the Llangollen Corwen Railway Company, Henry Robertson of Shrewsbury, had purchased land in Llandderfel and was having built a new mansion on the site where the old Pale Hall once stood. The following report on the 30th September highlights the welcome he received from the local inhabitant's:-

Welcome to Henry Robertson Esq.

At an early hour the inhabitants of Llandderfel were all astir, making preparations for a Gala Day. Most travellers by the Great Western Railway from Corwen to Bala have noticed near the Llandderfel station, that a new mansion was being erected on the site of the old Pale Hall, by Henry Robertson Esq., who has bought the estate. The old house, beautiful as it was with its clustering ivy, was not suited to modern taste and ideas - the inside being very inconvenient and badly arranged. Mr Robertson decided, reluctantly, but wisely, to remove the old house and build a new one on its site. The new mansion was designed by Mr Pountney Smith, architect, Shrewsbury, and is partly Elizabethan style.

By the 3 o' clock train a large number of people arrived both from Corwen and Bala and proceeded to the lodge, where a procession was formed headed by the Llandderfel Brass Band, followed by the children of the British and National Schools, the tenants four deep. As soon as the carriage in which Mr Henry Robertson Esq., Mrs Robertson, Miss Robertson, the Misses Robertson and Master Robertson, and Mr Beyer, came in sight, the band struck up "See the Conquering Hero Comes" and amid much cheering and firing of cannon, arrived at the Lodge where a tastefully erect and arch decorated by the foreman of the workers, a Mr C. Evans. Here, a large number of workmen took the horses from the carriage and pulled it joining the procession. The carriage was followed by hundreds of enthusiastic admirers of the family.

On arriving at the entrance hall the following address which had been beautifully engrossed on vellum by Messrs Mcgregor of Liverpool, was read by Rector W. Morgan and presented by Mr Thomas Jones, Pen-y-Bont as one of the oldest inhabitants.

In the address Mr Robertson was thanked for many public services which he hath rendered to the Principality and to this neighbourhood in particular, by the introduction of railways, by the advancement of education and progress of the working classes etc. Etc. Etc.

1872

Strike

This headline on March 16th 1872 mentions possibly the first ever strike on the local railway. The report goes on to state "This week we have again to announce another important strike which has occurred on the Great Western Railway. The platelayers have (from Dolgelley to Ruabon) absented themselves from their work owing to wages being low. The strike began at Corwen on Monday the 4th inst., and the platelayers have not yet recommenced work. We hope that the company and the platelayers will soon arrive at a definite arrangement.

Another fatality on the railway in the April, this time at Cynwyd Station:-

Fatal accident to a Baptist Minister at Cynwyd

It was reported that on the 15th inst. A Mr Edward Evans of Cynwyd, Baptist Minister aged 73 years, met with his death at Cynwyd Station.

When alighting from the train he fell between the platform and the rails, and was run over by two of the carriages. The inquest was held at the Cynwyd Railway Station. The jury returned a verdict of 'accidentally killed'.

A report on the evidence given by Sir Llewelyn Turner to the Parliamentary Committee on railway communications in North Wales in April 1872:-

Railway Communication in North Wales

Sir Llewelyn Turner of Carnarvon gave evidence on Friday before a Parliamentary Committee in favour of the scheme of the North Wales Narrow-Gauge Railway Company for the opening of the district between Corwen and Carnarvon and Portmadoc and Bettws-y-Coed by railway communication. He anticipated that if the railways were constructed an extensive trade would be created and that additional slate quarries will be worked.

Nothing was concluded.

The time-table of July 1872 shows for the first time two services operating on Sundays - one from Corwen departing at 9.25 a.m. arriving at London at 7.15 p.m. The second train departing from Dolgelley at 3.25 p.m., Corwen at 4.50 p.m. to arrive at Birmingham at 9.25 p.m., and by the August the Time-Table shows four through trains to London, two commencing from Dolgelley and two from Corwen.

However, by November, the Time-Table shows no Sunday trains were running on the Dolgelley to Corwen section. The only possible inference drawn here is that this was seasonal.

A fall of soil upon the Corwen - Llangollen line

A report in the C&DH on the 30th November, "A fall of soil upon the Corwen - Llangollen line obstructed the train. Passengers had to walk a few hundred yards into other trains which arrived from Ruabon.

It was said that it was fortunate that the fall was in daylight, as if this had occurred during darkness the consequences may have been serious.

The mount from which the soil had fallen was from Owain Glyndwr's mound outside of Carrog."

1873

In the January it was announced that two services from Corwen to London were operational at the beginning of 1873, and the journey times for these were as follows:-

Depart Corwen	Arrive London	Journey Time
8.05 a.m.	3.50 p.m.	7 ¾ hours
2.10 p.m.	10.40 p.m.	8 ½ hours

Another fatality at Cynwyd

In April it was reported that another fatality had occurred on the railway at Cynwyd when a Mr Robert Owen of Ty'n y Wern, on his way to Cynwyd Station at 7.40 p.m. was accidentally run over by the train at Llangar crossing, 200 yards away from Cynwyd.

Penarth Quarry one of the most profitable in the country

It was reported on the 2nd August that Penarth Quarry in its short period of operation, had become one of the most profitable in the whole country.

Due to its close proximity to Carrog Station, it was connected to the station by a new road through Carrog Afon farm and a new tramway.

Two tons of slate could be sent down by this means every 10 minutes. The workforce had now increased to 150.

Due to its close proximity to Llangollen-Corwen line, the slate could be delivered to most parts of England at special rates. It was also reported that, attracted by the complete success of operations at Penarth Quarry, new companies had commenced quarrying on the same vein upon the Berwyn Hills, one being Dee Side Quarry and the other a slate quarry on Moel Famau.

1874

Another fatal accident, this time at Corwen Station, the fourth since November 1866. The headline in the C&DH on the 19th September was as follows:-

Fatal accident to a breaksman

On Thursday September 10th at Corwen Station following the arrival of the 10.30 p.m. train from Ruabon, the breaksman, a Thomas Edwards, endeavoured to detach it. In the process, instead of going under the buffers to detach the wagon, he went between them, and consequently was squashed by them.

Accidents were on the increase, in this year alone, 80 passengers and 46 employees were killed in train accidents, and a total of 1298 railway personnel and members of the public were killed in stations and on the line.

1875

I take it that 1875 was a quiet year as no report of the Llangollen and Corwen railways appeared, neither in the 'Baner ac Amserau Cymru' nor the 'Carnarvon and Denbighshire Herald'.

1876

The marriage of Mr and Mrs Wynn, Rug.

The following report on the 30th September on the return of Mr and Mrs Wynn to Rug following their marriage, and the reception they received from their tenants and other residents at the Corwen railway station:-

Presentation of an illuminated address and tankard

In front of Corwen Station a commodious platform was erected upon a table thereon was placed a beautifully illuminated address and a magnificent silver tankard. Upon the tankard is artistically engraved the coat of arms of the Hon Mr Wynn (Hand and Boars Head) and the inscription "Presented to the Hon. C.H. Wynn of Rug, by his tenants and well wishers.

Upon arrival of the train from Ruabon, discharges of cannon and enthusiastic cheering greeted the happy pair, who were welcomed by the chairman and members of the committee, and escorted the Rug carriage close to the committee's platform, where the Rev. Mr Richardson, a rector of this Parish and chairman of the rejoicings committee made the following announcement - "*I have been requested to convey our warmest congratulations and our most cordial welcome home to Rug*" (loud cheers). The Squire and his lady were evidently touched by the heartiness of their welcome. The Rev. Richardson read the address and Mr Moltby, Ty Cerrig, presented the magnificent tankard which cost about 50 guineas.

The worthy Squire then returned a sensible speech and thanked everyone heartily. As they were all aware, that days reception was an honour that could only take place once in Mr and Mrs Wynn's life, and assured them that they would look back upon that reception which the people of Corwen had so spontaneously given as one of the most happiest days of their lives (loud cheering). He had to thank them again for the beautiful tankard which was a very acceptable present, by reminding them that when he came to live in Rug it was shorn of everything so that, that very handsome piece of silver would be a rich treasure in their home while it would be a record presented to them by their tenants and well wishers and with the address, recall at the same time the warm and enthusiastic welcome they had received coming home after their wedding tour. The grand procession was then formed. The horses were taken from the carriage, and scores of willing hands formed in line to draw the happy pair over Corwen bridge. 'The Bard of Snowdon' in melodious verse was sung "The ancient

Dee is a sacred river, it flows through a blesses land", echoed by at least three thousand voices of old and young. After night fall an exuberant display of fire balls took place in the Market Square in front of the well known Owain Glyndwr Hotel.

1877

Excursions

With the trains now in their heyday, the summer months would see a rush of people to seaside resorts. This was certainly true for many as the train had made it easier to travel to the coast. But spare a thought for people who lived on the coast as to where they would journey for their excursions! So perhaps it was not so unusual to find in the C&DH edition of the 14th July such advertisements detailing trips from Llandudno, Bangor and Conway to Bala Lake, Dolgelley, Llangollen and Corwen.

1878

Another quiet year. No reports of any kind were found.

1879

The following report on the 7th June perhaps details one of the more chilling experiences on the railway up to this period:-

Daring escape of a prisoner from the train

At the Petty Sessions held on the 31st ult., John Williams of Clawdd Newydd who had been discharged from Ruthin Gaol, sentenced for assaults on Police Officers, was charged by P.C.

William Jones for lodging in an out-house belonging to Dr Jones, Bala, and abusing and tearing the uniform of P.C. Tomos Jones who assisted in apprehending him. He was sentenced to 3 months hard labour at Ruthin Gaol. On being conveyed from Bala by train he made his daring escape. He has not been recaptured since. It appears when he left Bala he had both hands in handcuffs and was in the charge of P.C. Tomos Jones on the 4.45 train to Corwen.

Soon after leaving Bala station before entering the Ty-tan-y-graig tunnel, about 1 mile on the Bala side of Llandderfel station, the prisoner asked the officer to release the handcuff off the left wrist, pretending that they hurt him very much. The officer, with a display of kindness which was evidently undeserved, complied with this apparently reasonable request which was witnessed by passengers who were in the other compartments of the same carriage, whereupon the prisoner dealt the P.C. a heavy blow with the right hand to the wrist of which the pair of handcuffs was attached. In addition to his knowledge of this part of the line and surrounding countryside, the prisoner had another advantage in that the doors of the railway carriage were unlocked on both sides, he opened the carriage door, the officer tried to lay hold on him to stop him, whereby he ran the risk of being pulled down and injured. His helmet fell down and his prisoner made his escape in the tunnel while the train was moving at a rapid speed. As soon as the train arrived at Llandderfel station P.C. Jones, bareheaded, proceeded at once into the tunnel expecting to find the prisoner seriously injured if not killed, when to his surprise he had escaped apparently uninjured. The news of his escape was rapidly circulated, and officers from the different stations went in pursuit.

This report on the 23rd August emphasizes the vulnerability of the public to physical attacks on trains:-

Damages for assault

On Friday, Mr Sergeant Tindal Atkinson, County Court Judge, gave judgement in favour of William Peake, labourer and bailiff, against David Roberts, Coed Yale, Glyndyfrdwy, Corwen, farmer, for an assault committed in the Great Western Railway train between the stations of Berwyn and Glyndyfrdwy on the 25th of June last, for damages, court fees and costs amounting to 5/- (25p).

This report was in the C&DH edition 8th November:-

English Congregational Church

On Tuesday, Mr Thomas Barnes J.P. (the Quinta) Chairman of the Lancashire and Yorkshire Railway, laid the foundation stone of the English Congregational Church, Corwen. This Church was originated by a few Englishmen, chiefly connected with the railway service at Corwen. For several years they have met in a small assembly room in Brook Street, but were formed into a Congregational Church shortly after the North Wales English Congregational Union. Since then it has been under the fostering care of the Union, which has voted 50/- to the fund by Mr Hudson, the chairman of the Union. After the stone laying ceremony lunch was served at the Owain Glyndwr Hotel. The proceedings were most successful throughout.

1880, 1881, 1882

The papers are devoid of any reports for the years 1880, 1881 and 1882. Not even any time-tables appear to be available.

Corwen Station showing footbridge following dismantling of cover due to dilapidation.
Photo: Lens of Sutton

Cynwyd Station early 1900's with G.W.R. Steam Railmotor bound for Bala.
Photo: Lens of Sutton

Glyndyfrdwy Station was unusual in that it was located on an 'S' bend and trains approaching Up or Down would quickly disappear from view.

Photo: Lens of Sutton

Carrog Station on a quiet day in the 1950's.

Photo: Lens of Sutton

CHAPTER 5

STATION BUILDINGS

Corwen

Built by Mr Poultenay Smith of Shrewsbury, as well as being the largest intermediate station on the Ruabon to Barmouth length, Corwen was also a terminus for the L.N.W.R. / L.M.S. branch from Denbigh and Ruthin serving a central and hinterland population of some 4,000.

Although the station was owned by the G.W.R., both companies had through booking rights whereby the L.M.S. paid a proportional share of administrative costs including those of wages.

When the line was opened the main source of employment in the area was agriculture which also contributed to much of the railways' revenue. There doesn't appear to be available any drawing plans or documented evidence as to the layout of the original station, but it can be presumed that the main buildings were the original from 1865. The main buildings themselves were situated on the Down platform and were a mixture of stone and red brick consisting of the Station Master's Office, District Inspectors Office, booking office, parcels office, guards room, general waiting room, ladies waiting room, refreshment rooms and various store-rooms as well as two conveniences. At one time, towards the latter end of the 19th and early part of the 20th century, crockery was produced and sold bearing the name of Corwen Station and of the manufacturer, a J. W. Plack, and a bookstall was operated by

Wyman's on the Down platform, (photograph below) from the book 'Rails to Bala' (Southern, Leadbetter and Weatherley, - Charter Publications, 1987), although no date is mentioned.

As the largest station on the branch, Corwen boasted a bookstall operated by Wyman's. Photo: Charter Publications

Staff

The Slater's Directory dated 1868 in its chapter headed 'Conveyance by Railway on the Great Western and Denbigh Ruthin & Corwen Railways', a list of Station Master's for the stations in the district appears. A Mr Benjamin Buckton is listed as Station Master and Goods Agent for Corwen, Mr Isaac Roberts, Station Master for Gwyddelwern, Mr William Wellington, Station Master for Bryn and Derwen, Mr Thomas Williams, Station Master for Cynwyd, Mr Robert Roberts, Station Master for Llandrillo. The directory also mentions that an Omnibus from the White Lion, Bala, meets every train at Bala station.

Included in the Merionethshire Postal Directory of 1886 we

have what is believed to be the first complete or near-complete list of the staff employed at the station. A total of nineteen are listed but it must be assumed that this is not a comprehensive one and that some staff were possibly either omitted from the list or/and that some were also from the outlying areas and listed in the directory under their own towns/villages. Those mentioned are:- James Livesey, The Terrace, (Locomotive Superintendent); Samuel Morris, Railway Station, (Station Master); Thomas E. Parry, Bridge Street, (Railway Inspector); John Davies, Market Place, (Railway Inspector); Antony Appleton, School Terrace, (Engine Driver); Samuel Davies, Bridge Street, (Engine Driver); John Dickers, Glyndwr Terrace, (Engine Driver); David Jones, Woodbank, (Engine Driver); Charles Roberts, Union Terrace, (Engine Driver); James Smith, Glyndwr Terrace, (Engine Driver); Thomas Sparrow, Woodbank, (Engine Driver); Francis Croft, Woodbank, (Railway Guard); Robert Davies, Northyn Terrace, (Railway Guard); Richard Digby, Northyn Terrace, (Railway Guard); William Jones, Brynhyfryd, (Railway Guard); Robert Jones, Northyn Terrace, (Brakesman); John Roberts, Bridge Street, (Brakesman); William Jones, Northyn Terrace, (Pointsman); Thomas Jones, Mill Street, (Engine Cleaner).

A grave in the cemetry of St Mael & St Sulien Church in Corwen marks the burial place of one of the first train driver's from the area, that of Owen Owen who died in April 1872 aged 29. His epitaph is a fitting tribute to a train-driver and is reproduced on page 151.

In their book 'The Llangollen Line - Ruabon to Barmouth', W.G. Rear and N. Jones list the staff during the 1920's as consisting a Station Master (Class 2), Goods Clerk, 2 General Clerks, Junior Clerk, 2 Shunters, 4 Signalmen, Porter Signalman, Checker, Goods Porter, Parcels Porter, 1 Porter (Grade 1), 3 Porters (Grade 2) and a Junior Numbertaker. Further to these who were employed jointly between the G.W.R and the L.M.S., the G.W.R. also employed a District Inspector, 3 Goods Guards and 1 signalman. I'm a little unsure as to the requirements of a Junior Numbertaker, but accepting it was necessary, the time entailed for this task was so brief, then surely it must be assumed that the individual concerned would have additional duties to carry out.

Signal Boxes

There were two signal boxes, the East signal cabin being sited on the Up platform whilst the West box was situated on the Up-side of the running line near to Pont Corwen carrying the A5 over the River Dee. Both boxes were built of red-brick, the East box containing a frame with 34 levers whilst the smaller West box housed a 24 lever frame.

Electric Train-Staff

The East box had Electric Train Staff connection with Gwyddelwern on the L.M.S. (Corwen to Rhyl) line, and was connected via a telephone circuit to the Denbigh district. The West box controlled entry to the goods sidings on the West end and also marked the point at which resumption of the single-track main line followed on from the double track which covered the area between the two signal boxes and which was operated under double-line absolute block regulations. This system of signals was linked up by telegraph and telephone, which enabled the signalmen between the two boxes to communicate and warn each other of the approach of a train to any section of the line. No passenger train was allowed on to a section if another train was already on it, and this system was known as the block system, because by it a train was blocked or prevented from leaving a section until the next section was clear. Although the distance covered by Corwen East to West boxes was but about three hundred yards, a block section varied and could be anything up to five miles in length.

In its early days a system of hand signals and flags were used but these soon gave way to mechanical signals of various types. It is most likely that the first system deployed at Corwen would have been that of a disc and crossbar signal (see illustration - right) which operated in such a way that the disc and crossbar were mounted on a spindle at right-angles to each other so that one or the other was always displayed to the driver, the disc indicating 'all clear'. Invented by the great engineer of the Great Western Railway, Isambard Brunel, the very distinctive disc and crossbar type of signal was much in advance of some contemporaries. Lacking the luxury of a ladder for maintenance men to attend to lamps and oil the bearings, this task was achieved by small notches cut into the post to provide a foothold to ascend the posts up to 50ft high.

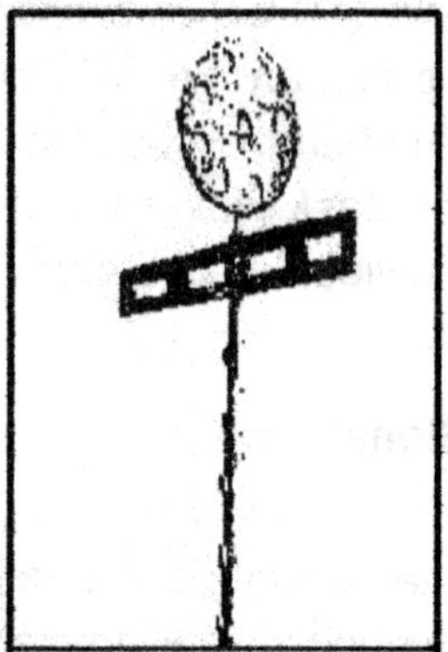

A disc signal and crossbar.

On the G.W.R. line (Corwen to Llangollen) the East signal box had Electric Train Staff connection with Carrog and Key Token Equipment with Glyndyfrdwy when Carrog was switched out.

Other Buildings

Advertisements found in the Suttons Directory of 1881 list two builders' merchant's having their premises on land belonging to and adjacent to the railway, these being Edward Jones and W.F. Jones and Hughes, the latter being also a steam saw mill and coal merchant. In addition to the buildings mentioned there was also at one time a corrugated iron motor garage adjoining the station. To the west of the station and on the Down side there was a goods shed, a crane, cattle pens and permanent way stores. As well as being a location for the coal merchant a local Farmer's Association had their office and warehouse situated on the Down side and later constructed another rail-served warehouse opposite to the West signal-box, whilst on the Up side there was a locomotive shed located to the rear of the West signal-box as well as a 55ft Turntable.

Locomotive Shed

This was located on the Up side on the Ruabon end of the site and the building itself located behind the West Signal Box. A 55ft turntable was provided and alongside this was a pillar tank supplying colums at the Ruabon end of the Up platform, the Barmouth end of the Down platform and the one situated outside the Locomotive shed.

The shed fell victim to G.W.R.'s decision to close it in 1927 and the deployment of seven sets of G.W.R. men based at Corwen saw the transfer of the workforce to Bala, Croesnewydd (Wrexham) and Penmaenpool.

In addition to the G.W.R., the L.M.S. who had three sets of men outstationed at Corwen, were unwilling to continue the workings of the shed and consequently its workforce was transferred to Denbigh. In addition to driver's, firemen and guards, there were also locomotive and carriage cleaners, but how many is not clearly known.

For a couple of years following the closure of the locomotive shed the traffic department retained its freight guards although the passenger guards were transferred before 1930.

The goods yard which was located on the Down side at the Barmouth end of the station where siding accommodation comprised of five sidings giving a storage capacity for 115 wagons; of these the cattle-pen siding had a capacity for 20. Two sidings on the Up-side had a capacity for 38 wagons; these were the West-end No.1 siding housing 28 wagons and was the shunting spur whilst No. 2 siding housed 10 wagons. The warehouse on the Down-side housed 4 wagons. There were two cranes contained within the building each with a lifting capacity of 30cwts. and had a load-gauge installed. Together with a weighbridge in the mileage yard there was a yard crane with a lifting capacity of 8 tons.

SERVICES

Time-Tables

Some publications have listed that the earliest available official time-table for Corwen appears to be the Denbigh Ruthin & Corwen Railway Time-Table for November 1867, this being taken from the "Douglas North Wales Railways Time Tables". However, the Carnarvon & Denbigh Herald and North and South Wales Independent list a Vale of Clwyd, Denbigh Ruthin and Corwen Railway Time-Table in its edition of Saturday 8th October 1864, and this must without doubt be the first one ever for any train journey both out of and in to Corwen as it is dated as from 22nd September 1864, the very day the line itself had been opened. (see page 34 for time-table).

The efficiency of time-tables must be questioned in the early days of the railway, as twenty-six years prior to the opening of the Corwen line it was stated that the reason that no proper time-tables were issued in the early days was as explained by a Charles Saunders to the Parliamentary Committee on Railways in April 1841, *"At the opening in 1838 we found the engines were so inefficient that time-table working was hopeless; one or two engines might keep time, the other eight or ten were always out of time"*. We must presume that by the 1860's there must have been some improvement as there does not appear to be any reference to inefficiency of time-tabling.

PASSENGER AND FREIGHT WORKINGS

Denbigh Ruthin and Corwen

The earliest available Time-Table on the Denbigh Ruthin & Corwen Railway, as stated above, appears in the Carnarvon & Denbigh Herald in its issue for 8th October 1864, this being 17 days after its opening to passenger traffic. A total of four through passenger trains to Rhyl and four from Rhyl operated daily with the first train departing Corwen at 8.08 a.m. with arrival scheduled at Rhyl for 10.00 a.m. A year on from its opening the number of passenger through trains to Rhyl was down to two with the first train departing at 8.00 a.m. and the second at 11.30 a.m., although four through trains ran through to Corwen from Rhyl, but by the November this had decreased to three. This had all changed considerably by December however, with four through trains both ways, the first departure being 8.15 a.m from Corwen with subsequent services at 11.20 a.m., 1.55 p.m. and 4.50 p.m. At this time there were no separate services from Corwen to Ruthin.

By January 1875 the first train departed at 7.30 a.m. to Denbigh, 10.35 a.m. through to Chester, 2.40 p.m. and 5.20 p.m. to Denbigh. Only three trains by this period worked to Corwen; 7.20 a.m. from Chester, 12.00 p.m. and 3.40 p.m. from Denbigh.

In the July of 1904 issue of the 'Working Time-Table', five passenger and one freight worked through to Corwen with the same number of departures, and with slight variations in timings only, the services remained broadly the same until after the First World War. Even following the formation of the London Midland Scottish Railway Company in 1923 there was little change in traffic patterns. The first significant reduction in passenger service was caused by the General Strike of 1926 with time-tables showing three passenger trains operating each way between Corwen and Denbigh. By the following year however, there was an increase to six passenger services each way between Corwen and Denbigh. A change to the mode of operation occurred at about this time in that the majority of trains from Corwen ran through to Chester.

In its heyday during the 1930's, seventeen trains operated each way during summer weekdays, which had increased from nine each way in 1900, although not all these worked through to Corwen.

L.M.S. Country Lorry Services

The majority of through trains from the Denbigh L.M.S. line to Corwen made connection with the Great Western through trains. As Corwen marked the terminus of the L.M.S. branch from Rhyl, the company established a unique practice by which to compete against the G.W.R. for local passenger services. They operated L.M.S. Country Lorry Services and were at one period a regular feature in the area, serving the outlying villages of Betws Gwerfil Goch, Carrog, Cerrig-y-Drudion, Cynwyd, Glanrafon, Llandrillo and Maerdy.

Ironically, it was in the summer of 1939 just prior to the outbreak of the Second World War that the zenith of the line's history was reached. In addition to the six daily trains in each direction, two trains to Corwen were added to the time-table for Wednesdays and Saturdays.

Although not as severe as the cuts experienced by other branch-lines, the Denbigh Ruthin and Corwen saw a reduction in its services at the outbreak of the war in September 1939, but by the October of 1940 the service had once again increased to five passenger trains. During the 1948 season an extra passenger train was added to the Rhyl - Corwen time-table at 2100 on Saturdays.

Although regular passenger trains had ceased on 2nd February 1953, it was on 30th April 1962 that the line closed to all traffic by which time the turntable had also been decommissioned, necessitating locomotives to work tender-first one way.

One of the L.M.S. country bus services which operated from Corwen station in the early 1900's serving the outlying villages of Betws Gwerfil Goch, Carrog, Cerrig-y-Drudion, Cynwyd, Glanrafon, Llandrillo and Maerdy.

Photo: Jim Roberts

Corwen Station and staff early 1900's. Photo: Lens of Sutton

Ruabon - Barmouth

In the mid-1870's Corwen's first link with Paddington was formed. The 1000 out of Paddington arrived at Barmouth at 1841 with a change at Ruabon. Unfortunately, I have not been able to establish the arrival time at Corwen as no time-table for the period can be located. By the turn of the century the journey time between Paddington and Barmouth had improved by approximately an hour with the 0950 from Paddington arriving at its terminus at 1750.

By 1907 the section from Ruabon to Corwen West remained open continuously, the only exception being between the hours of 0530 to 1730 on Sundays. A class K goods train departed from Ruabon daily at 0045 arriving at Corwen at 0210. The lengthy journey-time was due to a 20 minute stop at Glyndyfrdwy. It's not certain why there was this lengthy stop but I believe it could well have been for loading slate wagons as there was a slate siding at Glyndyfrdwy with a capacity for 10 wagons, and as the Moel Fferna slate quarries contributed to much of the goods traffic, this appears to be the most likely explanation. It is also probable that coal was unloaded as there was a coal-yard in its early days to the rear of the Up-side. The track from Glyndyfrdwy to the slate quarries was a 2ft gauge Deeside tramway.

The first ever through working to Dolgellau was a Class F Freight departing Ruabon at 0420 running non-stop to Corwen where there was a 13 minute wait before resuming its journey to Bala Junction and finally arriving at Dolgellau at 0625. The first Down passenger departed Ruabon at 0750 and arriving at Dolgellau at 0945 having stopped at all stations, and in all there were 5 daily passenger through trains.

Further services on Sundays included 2 freight workings, the 0045 Ruabon to Corwen and the 0420 Ruabon to Dolgellau with two motor train workings between Ruabon and Corwen. On the Up-line the first train of the day departed Corwen at 0220, stopping at the gradient board at Acrefair in order to pin down brakes and arriving at Ruabon at 0315. A total of four passenger workings between Dolgellau and Ruabon, the last daily through working being the mail train departing Dolgellau at 1935 arriving at Ruabon at 2142.

Although there were no through Goods workings there were three daily Goods departures from Dolgellau to Corwen, with the majority of duties being worked by Corwen Locomotive Department prior to G.W.R.'s decision to close the shed in 1927.

It appears that the period intervening the two World Wars was the most active one of the railways' history. By this time a total of 2½ hours had been clipped off the 1870's timings on the original Paddington to Barmouth run, departing the former at 9.10 a.m. and arriving at its terminus at 3.21 p.m. Six weekday journeys were made by the Ruabon to Llangollen shuttle, five from Ruabon to Dolgellau and two Ruabon to Corwen. Of these, an Omnibus took passengers between Llangollen and Corwen on both Thursday and Saturday in addition to which there were afternoon road motor trips between Corwen and Dolgellau. Of the three Sunday shuttles between Ruabon and Llangollen, two continued to Corwen by road, but at the outbreak of World War Two, Sunday services were terminated.

GWYDDELWERN STATION & BUILDINGS

The most significant historical part of the railway in Gwyddelwern is that it was the first fully-operational station in the Vale of Edeyrnion, receiving its first services on Thursday 22nd September 1864, when the whole of the Ruthin to Corwen section was opened. As the temporary terminus on the Corwen end of the Denbigh, Ruthin & Corwen railway, it even boasted at one time its own engine-shed. According to the Slater's Directory for 1868, its Station Master at this time was a Mr Isaac Roberts, and it is more than likely that he was the first at Gwyddelwern taking into account that the station was only four years into service.

Gwyddelwern Station Photo: H. C. Casserley

The most significant historical part of the railway in Gwyddelwern is that it was the first fully-operational station in the Vale of Edeyrnion, receiving its first services on Thursday 22nd September 1864, when the whole of the Ruthin to Corwen section was opened. As the temporary terminus on the Corwen end of the Denbigh, Ruthin & Corwen railway, it even boasted at one time its own engine-shed. The first Station Master was Mr Isaac Roberts.

A distance of 2 miles 980 yards from Corwen and 9 miles 1104 yards from Ruthin, Gwyddelwern station consisted of a single platform on the Down side of the track with a goods loop on the Up side. As with other stations on the line, a canopy was fitted over the platform. On the Corwen end of the platform was a small 4-lever frame controlling signals, and also a horse-loading bay. To the rear of the station buildings were cattle pens and a weigh-machine. At the Denbigh end there was a coal siding and weigh machine from which a second siding ran parallel to the main line.

The steep climb from Corwen to Gwyddelwern continued towards Denbigh for approximately 1 mile, with the highest part being 620 feet above sea-level. A little further on there were two quarries, both having their own sidings, these being Dee Clwyd Granite Quarry, commenced in 1891, and the Craig-Lelo Quarry, commencing in 1924. Access to both sidings was controlled from a ground frame locked by the train staff. Much of the station's revenue came from the quarries.

It may have been the first operational station in the Vale of Edeyrnion, but it was also the first to close to both passenger and goods traffic. Passenger services were withdrawn on 2nd February 1953 and goods traffic ceased on 2nd December 1957.

GLYNDYFRDWY STATION & BUILDINGS

The station itself was nestled between the village and the river Dee. It had a crossing and a token exchange station connecting with Llangollen Goods Line Junction toward Ruabon when Deeside Loop was switched out, and then on the Corwen side with Carrog or Corwen East. The main station building, on the Down side, was built of stone which had built into it the Station Master's house. Other main buildings on the Down side were a Booking Office, General Waiting Room, Ladies Waiting Room, two conveniences and a corrugated sheet lamp hut.

The Waiting Room on the Up platform was constructed of Ruabon red-brick as was the base of the signal-box which was also sited on this side. Built in 1898, the signal box had 24 levers and also controlled the level-crossing at the Ruabon end, and this replaced the original signal box constructed in 1877.

Beyond the level crossing on the Down side was a small yard with two sidings accessed by a small two lever ground frame locked by a key on the Electric Train Staff. The No. 1 siding had a capacity to hold 13 wagons and had a load gauge over it. The No. 2 siding held 9 wagons and a had truck weighbridge. The Moelferna Slate Quarries provided most of the traffic from the station. In addition to the above the goods yard also contained a cart weighbridge where there was a small warehouse and a crane with a 3 ton lifting capacity. In 1925 a total of five staff were employed: a Class 5 Station Master, three signalmen, (one who was also employed at Deeside Loop) and a porter signalman. The main revenue at this time was Goods which was double the passenger receipts.

Of the main buildings on the Down side were a Booking Office, General Waiting Room, Ladies Waiting Room, two conveniences and a corrugated sheet lamp hut.

CARROG STATION & BUILDINGS

The main buildings were on the Up side and consisted of a Booking Office, General Waiting Room, Ladies Waiting Room with toilet, Gentlemen's toilet and a lamp room. Contained within the stone-built structure was a Station Master's house. Also on the Up platform was a signal-box which housed a frame of 20 levers controlling all points and signals. The Down platform contained a General Waiting Room and a toilet, all construction being of Ruabon red brick. A total of 3 staff were employed: a Class 5 Station Master and two porter signalmen.

Token Equipment was provided and the sections were to Glyndyfrdwy and to Corwen East box. Although provided with a crossing loop and Token Equipment it was rarely used for that purpose. The track layout consisted of a loop with the entry road in line with the main line. Facing Corwen bound trains was a two arm bracket signal which controlled access to the small yard on the Up side which contained two sidings with a capacity for 45 wagons. Livestock being the principal freight traffic, the smaller siding provided a horse landing and cattle pens for this purpose, although it must be noted that general goods, lime, coal and timber were handled regularly over a number of years. A small goods warehouse, situated on the Up platform contained a cart weighbridge, but only Down direction freight trains picked up or set down in the yard.

A feature of Carrog station was a Camping Coach in the siding, which were popular holiday destinations during the late 1940's and 1950's.

There is no sign of a siding for Penarth Quarry which would have been on the Down side.

CYNWYD STATION & BUILDINGS

A small station in comparison to its counterparts within Edeyrnion, consisting on the Down side a single platform and one siding with a capacity for 28 wagons. The siding passed through a Goods Warehouse which was 36 feet in length. A load gauge was provided over the siding and there was a cart weighbridge in the yard. Behind the platform there were cattle pens and at each end of the siding were ground frames, East and West, locked by the key on the Electric Train Staff.

As with most stations, the main buildings were constructed of Ruabon red brick and these comprised of a Booking Office, General Waiting Room, Ladies Waiting Room and two conveniences. The Station Master's house was located, not within the complex of the station itself, but in the village.

In addition to the Station Master Class 5 the station employed a gatewoman as well as a porter who also attended to the lamps at Corwen, Llandrillo and Llandderfel.

The Electric Train Staff was collected at Corwen West where the single line resumed for the section between Corwen West and Llandrillo. Following the course of the river Dee for most of the way, much of the section was on a rising gradient of 1 in 200.

A short distance from Corwen West a minor road crossed at Llangar Church which was provided with block indicators located in a cottage situated at the side of the line. The cottage was rented out to a railway lengthman whose wife attended the crossing for which duties she received the sum of 4/- (20 p) per week, of which

2/- (10p) was deducted for rent - these figures relate only to a period in the 1920's as no other figures are available. Although closer to Corwen, the crossing came under the supervision of the Cynwyd Station Master.

LLANDRILLO STATION & BUILDINGS

A distance of 2½ miles from Cynwyd, Llandrillo station was provided with a crossing loop on the Down side. The main buildings, also located on the Down side, comprised a Booking Office, General Waiting Room, Ladies Waiting Room and two conveniences. The Station Master's house was located in the Goods Yard to the rear of the signal box. A General Waiting Room

Of the stations in the Vale of Edeyrnion, Llandrillo's was the one which was furthest from its own village centre than any other, a distance of approximately ¾ mile. The first Station Master was a Mr Robert Roberts.

Llandrillo Station in the early 1900's. Photo: Lens of Sutton

and two conveniences were situated on the Up side. The only access to the Up platform from the Down side was at the foot of the platform ramps on the Corwen end where a series of sleepers provided a crossing for both passengers and parcels. I presume it was a safe means of crossing as British Railways must have operated a dual procedure for these sleeper crossings; on most such crossings there would be 'Trespassers will be Prosecuted' notices and only parcels would be allowed to be carried across. Originally intended for transporting goods and mail from one platform to the other, it had this further use in allowing passengers to cross on those stations which did not have a footbridge.

The signal box was located on the Down platform and housed a frame of 24 levers, 6 of which were spare. The Goods Yard consisted of a loop with a capacity for 25 wagons. The No. 1 siding could accomodate 9 wagons with No. 2 having a capacity for 29. In the Goods Yard a small corrugated iron warehouse was located which had a crane with a 1 ton lifting capacity, and there was a loading gauge over No. 1 siding.

Only three staff were employed at Llandrillo, a Station Master Class 5 and two Class 5 signalmen with the Cynwyd porter attending to the lamps and other station duties as and when necessary. As was the case with other stations in the area, the revenue from goods traffic was approximately double that of the returns on Passengers.

Of the stations in the Vale of Edeyrnion, Llandrillo was the one which was furthest from its own village centre than any other, a distance of approximately ¾ mile, although at one time it was contemplated to build Corwen's station at Tyn-y-Cefn, which would have been further still from its town centre.

BONWM HALT

Extraordinary as it may sound, Bonwm was built in G.W.R.'s attempt to increase traffic. This was in the 1920's and the name itself was taken from the small hamlet which was located on the A5 mid-way between Corwen and Carrog. The platform was a little over seventy feet in length with a wooden shelter for passengers. It had the wooden nameboard erected on the platform together with one electric lamp which the guard of the passing train was required to switch on and off as necessary. A drivers skill was honed to perfection as he was required to stop with the Guard's Van at the platform. Not all services were required to stop at the halt, this was shown to be conditional upon the needs of passengers.

Bonwm Halt Photo: P. Baughan

The guard would collect the initial fare either Down to Corwen or Up to Carrog, and then informing the booking clerk there of passenger details who would then be re-booked to their relevant destinations. The halt remained in service until the final day of operations in 1964.

TRACK MAINTENANCE

All track renewal and maintenance on single line involved total line occupation, and subsequently confined to night time and Sundays. Careful planning ensured that the locomotive was suitably placed to enable relief crews to change over during the day. It was also necessary to ensure that locomotives had adequate water supply to last the shift.

CORONATION LAND CRUISE

The first 'Land Cruise' excursions were seen in 1951 during the 'Festival of Britain' year and were reintroduced in 1953 as the 'Coronation Land Cruise' and were familiar sights on Corwen station throughout the 1950's. These commenced in Rhyl and would arrive in Corwen via Denbigh and Ruthin where they joined the G.W.R. section bound for Dolgellau and Barmouth. The excursion would then continue along the Cambrian Coast to Afonwen and through to Caernarfon and Bangor to complete its round trip back to Rhyl.

These excursions proved to be so popular that another was introduced in 1954 commencing from Llandudno and from Rhyl incorporating the same itinerary as the 1953 cruises. By 1954 demand was growing and further trains were introduced to meet this. It was during this year that an excursion started from Pwllheli working along the coast to Barmouth, then across the Mawddach estuary to head inland as far as Corwen. From here it continued through the Vale of Clwyd to Rhyl and along the north coast to Caernarfon and Afonwen. The round trip was completed as the journey continued to Pwllheli.

By 1955 the 'Land Cruise' excursion operated from Monday to Friday and by 1956 a variation to the excursion was introduced. This extended the cruise on the Llandudno run by journeying south from Barmouth Junction to Aberdovey and returning via Afonwen and Caernarfon to Llandudno and did not venture inland as previously. The Pwllheli Land Cruise however continued inland and through to Corwen.

The summer of 1959 saw another revision of the Land Cruise using Rhyl once more as a starting point travelling west-wards to Caernarfon and Criccieth having travelled over Pant Glas summit, before descending to the Cambrian Coast through Afonwen. As in previous years it crossed the Mawddach estuary and through Dolgellau to take water at Corwen. These stops were short at Corwen but always allowed time enough for passengers to purchase from the on-platform refreshment room.

By 1960 the Rhyl-starting Land Cruise that took in Corwen was re-named '*The Welsh Chieftain*', whilst the Llandudno one was re-named '*The Clwyd Ranger*' and took in Corwen with a 35-minute stop. However, by this time it operated on Tuesdays and Wednesdays only, and unfortunately, this was the last year for the Land Cruise to be seen in Corwen.

ROUTE OF THE

CORONATION LAND CRUISE 1953

The following brief notes are given to help the traveller identify the principal points of interests on the route. The tour is divided into four sections - Rhyl to Corwen, Corwen to Barmouth, Barmouth to Afonwen and Afonwen to Rhyl. All references are given looking ahead, that is, facing the direction of travel.

SECTION 2 —

Corwen to Barmouth

The train stops for a few minutes at Corwen, a small market town where Glendower had his headquarters and where he assembled his forces before the battle of Shrewsbury. Beyond Corwen, the valley of the Dee, which increases in beauty as we ascend, is known as the Vale of Edeyrnion. Passing Bala Junction the peaceful market town of Bala is seen a short distance away to the right, and the train is soon running alongside Bala Lake. The lake ("Llyn Tegid" in Welsh) is 3¼ miles long , ¾ mile broad, and 530 feet deep, and, with the foothills covered with heather, ferns and scattered trees and the great mountain of Arenig Fawr (2,800 ft.) behind, possesses a singular charm in clear and sunny weather. To our left as we proceed, Aran Benllyn (2,901 ft.) comes boldly into view at the end of its long ridge. The line ascends through a desolate region, overshadowed by Aran Benllyn, to its highest point (770 feet). The descent is rapid to Drws-y-Nant and through the Valley of Wnion, crossing and recrossing the impetuous stream amid some of the most delightful sylvan scenes in Wales. The cliffs of Cader Idris (2,927 ft.) with the steep face of Tyrau Mawr, rise directly ahead to our left as we approach Dolgelley, the capital of Merionethshire. Owen Glendower held a Welsh Parliament at Dolgelley in 1404, and in the following year signed his allegiance with Charles VI of France. The town manufactures woollen goods, but is chiefly noted as a tourist resort owing to its singularly beautiful situation. Our route now runs alongside the Mawddach Estuary, with its splendid views of Cader Idris range on the left. The Afon Maddach is crossed by a long railway bridge, and we arrive at Barmouth, where time is allowed to enjoy the glorious views.

With the Compliments of

BRITISH RAILWAYS

Reproduction of the poster for the Coronation Land-Cruise of 1953.

There appears to be an error in the advertisement as it states that Owen Glendower (Owain Glyndwr) held a Welsh Parliament at Dolgelley (Dolgellau), but as far as I'm aware this was at Machynlleth. It's possible that this was 'commercial licence' on behalf of British Railways.

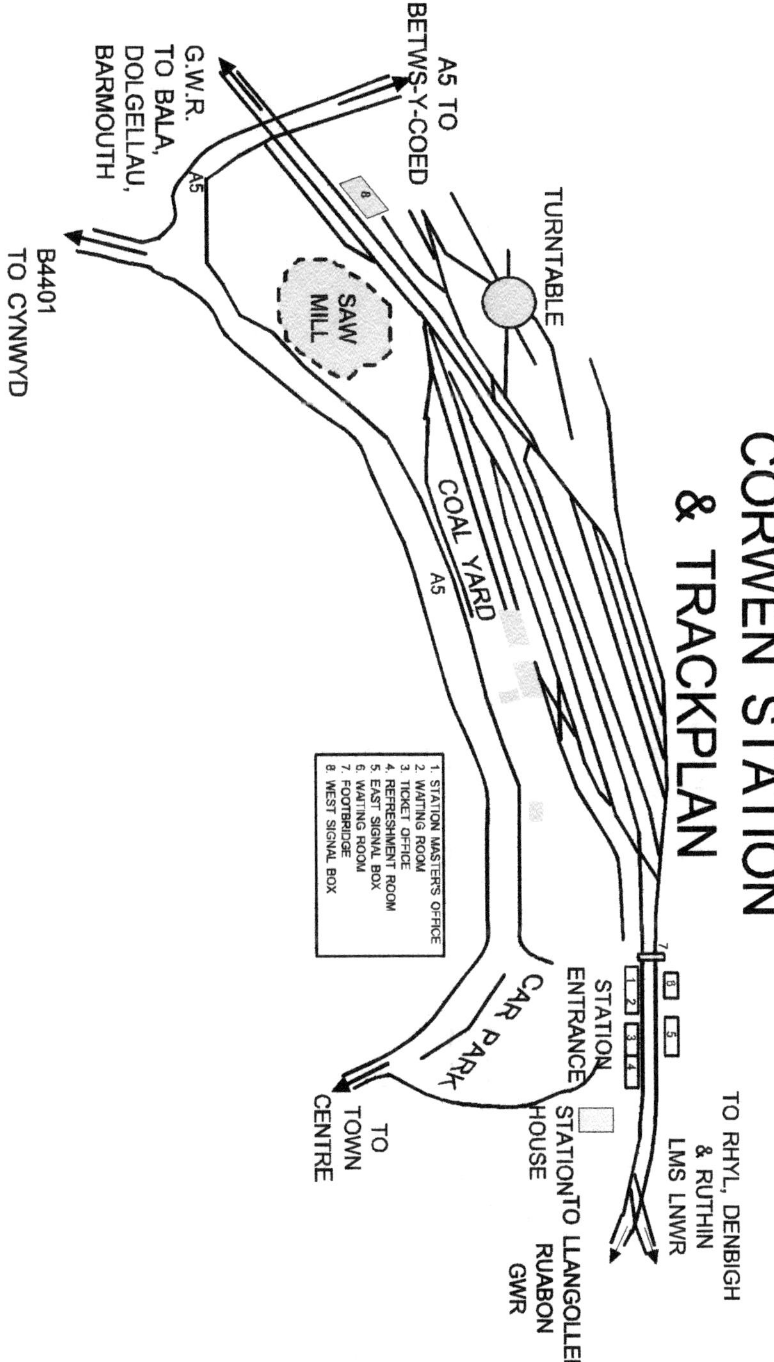
CORWEN STATION
& TRACKPLAN
A5 TO
BETWS-Y-COED
G.W.R.
TO BALA,
DOLGELLAU,
BARMOUTH
A5
B4401
TO CYNWYD
TURNTABLE
SAW
MILL
COAL YARD
A5
1. STATION MASTER'S OFFICE
2. WAITING ROOM
3. TICKET OFFICE
4. REFRESHMENT ROOM
5. EAST SIGNAL BOX
6. WAITING ROOM
7. FOOTBRIDGE
8. WEST SIGNAL BOX
STATION
ENTRANCE
CAR PARK
TO
TOWN
CENTRE
STATION
HOUSE
TO LLANGOLLEN,
RUABON
GWR
TO RHYL, DENBIGH
& RUTHIN
LMS LNWR

GWYDDELWERN STATION & TRACKPLAN

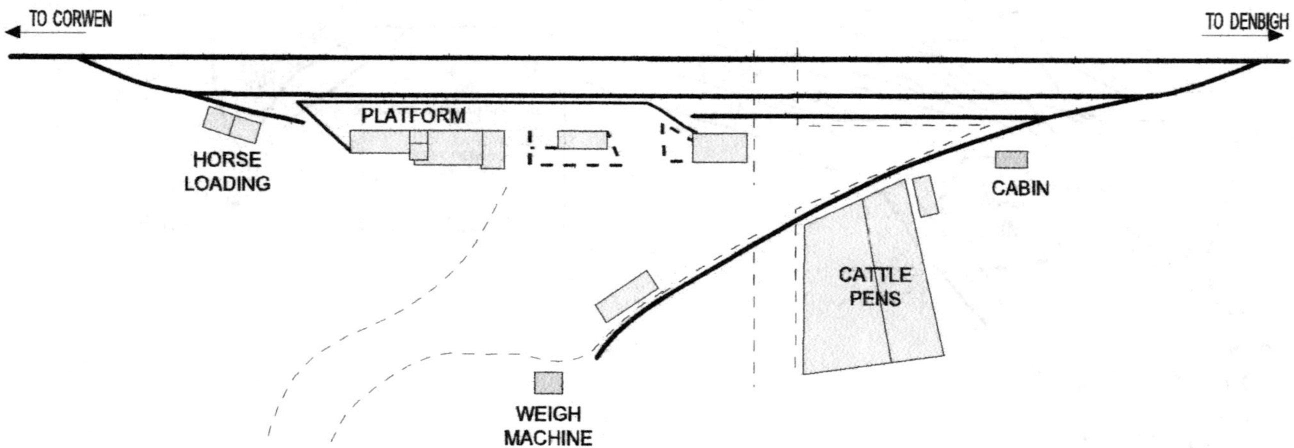

GLYNDYFRDWY STATION & TRACKPLAN

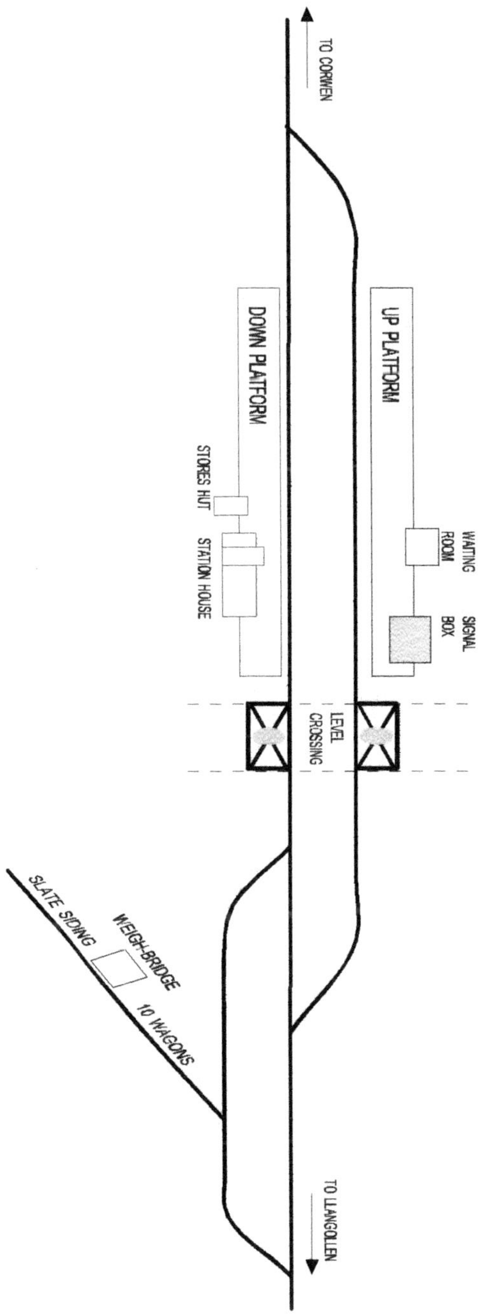

CARROG STATION & TRACKPLAN

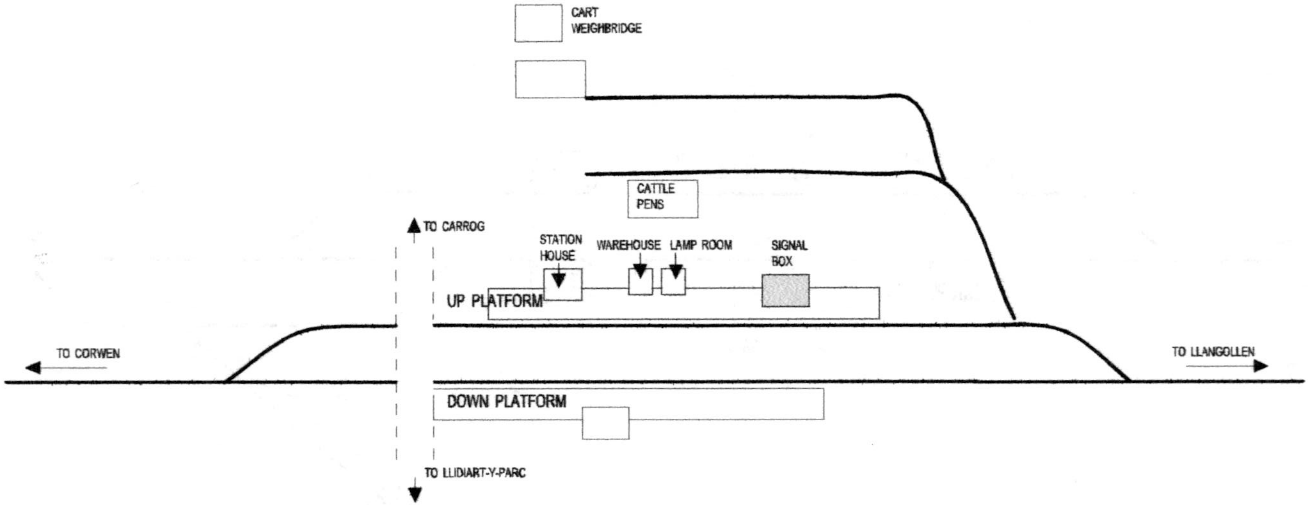

CYNWYD STATION & TRACKPLAN

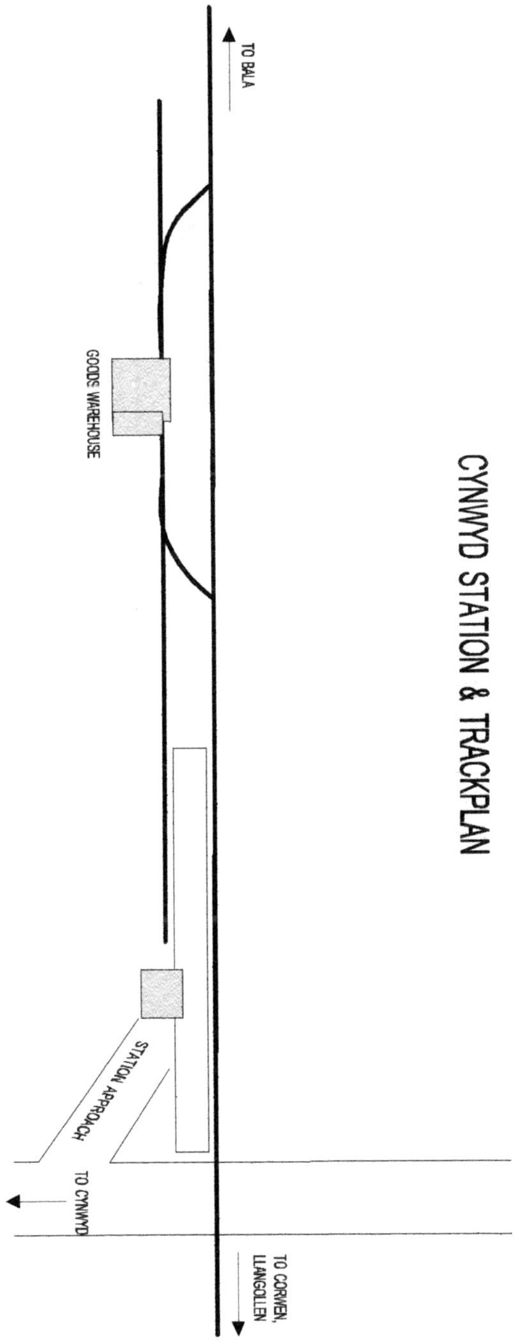

LLANDRILLO STATION & TRACKPLAN

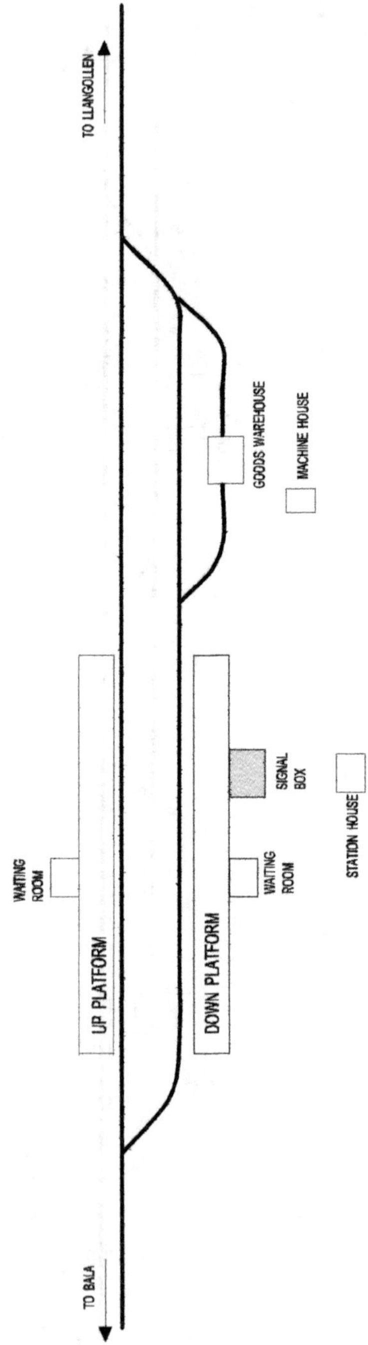

CHAPTER 6

ENGINEERS & CONTRACTORS

Before the railways, canals were the chief means of carrying heavy goods. These were principally constructed in the latter half of the 18th century and the first half of the 19th century. It was from the Llangollen section of the Shropshire Union Canal that much of the area's crop production was transported to other parts of the country, but much, if not most of its livestock was taken by drovers. The volume and frequency of goods transportation placed great reliance on an inadequate road network. With the growth of industry it became inevitable that an alternative mode of transport was required. Although transport costs via canal were less than half those by road and of the newest canals, unless they had a special Act of Parliament the canal companies were unable to act as carriers. The intention of this Act was to prevent the creation of a transport monopoly. In areas where all available transport systems were operating to capacity, little incentive was provided for contractors to undercut rivals nor indeed to minimize journey-time. What this meant was that merchandise took longer to travel the 30 canal miles from Liverpool to Manchester than it took to sail across the Atlantic. And so the second-half of the 19th century witnessed unparalleled progress in networking a railway system.

Railways the length and breadth of the United Kingdom owe much to the achievements of engineers and contractors. It comes as no surprise therefore that as such, the honour of the railway age was mostly attributed to them.

The engineers notable for their efforts in bringing the age of the railway to the Corwen area were Henry Robertson of Shrewsbury, engineer for the Llangollen & Corwen Railway Company and Benjamin and Robert Piercy of Welshpool for the Denbigh, Ruthin and Corwen Railway Company.

Having put up the Parliamentary deposit for the Bill, David Davies of Llandinam and Thomas Savin were appointed contractors to the Piercy brothers whilst Thomas Brassey of Chester was assigned the same post to assist Henry Robertson.

Achievements of Henry Robertson

Possibly overshadowed by such renowned engineers of the 19th century as Brunel and Stephenson, the achievements of Henry Robertson were somewhat unfairly rendered insignificant by comparison. The Dee Viaduct on the Shrewsbury & Chester built in 1848 is 1,508 ft in length, 147 ft high with 19 arched spans bears testament to his ingenuity. A little over 2 miles to the south of the viaduct he constructed another viaduct to cross the Ceiriog Valley at Chirk, this being 846 ft in length with ten intermediate stone arches and reaching 106 ft at its highest point is another monument to his skill. He was later knighted and also became the Member of Parliament for Shrewsbury. For some period he lived at Crogen Hall between the villages of Llandrillo and Llandderfel and also at Pale Hall in Llandderfel.

David Davies

One of the most remarkable of the early pioneers of the South Wales coalfields and leading railway contractor in Wales was David Davies of Llandinam. He tendered and won his first contract to construct the Llanidloes to Newtown in 1853. His impression upon the directors of that railway was being awarded the contract for the second section of that line, reaching Llandinam in 1856 and its completion to Newtown in 1859.

He was contracted to build the Denbigh, Ruthin & Corwen Railway, work on this commencing in 1860 and its completion came about four years later.

A self-made man, he had made his way by the shrewd use of money he had acquired by his own hard work. However, it was not before risking thirty thousand pounds in the sinking of coal-pits in the Rhondda Valley that he made his real fortune.

Thomas Brassey

A person of no less importance was his contractor on the Llangollen Corwen railway, Thomas Brassey. At one time Brassey's total labour force employed in both the United Kingdom and various parts of mainland Europe was 45,000. In Britain alone he undertook the construction of 1700 route miles of railway whilst abroad he was responsible for 2800 route miles as far afield as Canada. Amongst his many other ventures was the construction of Chester station. During the 1860's there were many reports of contractors becoming bankrupt and the collapse in May 1866 of Overend, Gurney and Co. (who financed the Stockton and Darlington railway) led to Thomas Brassey losing over £1 million.

Benjamin and Robert Piercy

The Piercy brothers came into prominence in the Mid-Wales region and together with contractors David Davies and Thomas Savin, planned and constructed railways from Llanidloes through to Newtown and Oswestry.

In 1856 Benjamin and Robert Piercy commenced work on the Vale of Clwyd Railway from Rhyl to Ruthin. Initially, David Davies was the sole contractor, but when funds had finally dried up on the Mid-Wales projects, he was joined by his partner Thomas Savin.

CHAPTER 7

NAVVIES

So much has been documented remarking upon the achievements of the engineers and contractors, but sadly very little has been mentioned of the contribution of the navvy. Railways surely were built not only by engineers, contractors, machines, etc., but also navvies, who contributed more in terms of employed labour, man hours, and suffered far more tragic fatalities.

The name 'navvies' was derived from those who had built the river navigations, and were known in some parts of Britain as 'navvies' or 'navigators'. The earliest form of spelling was 'navey' (plural 'naveys') and during the 1850's changed to 'navvy' (plural 'navvies').

One of Robert Stephenson's assistant engineers, a Lieutenant Peter Lecount, referred to the navvies as 'banditti' as they were generally the terror of the surrounding country and that they were completely a class by themselves very much the same as Gipsies.

How accurate this statement made by Lecount cannot be substantiated, therefore some doubt must be cast upon what can only be termed as probably no more than a hysterical outburst against the working-classes. It appears that the 'higher orders' of society exhausted their fury in condemning the navvy for his rebelliousness so much so that they were left with nothing to berate the shareholder's, engineers and contractors for their lack of compassion towards the injuries and fatalities suffered by the navvies. This was not true of all the 'upper echelon' however, as the chairman of the Llangollen Corwen Railway, Colonel Tottenham, paid a great compliment to the navvies employed on that line, and to *".... bear witness to the excellent conduct, generally speaking, of all the men engaged on the line. They had been engaged for two winters through about five miles of my property where I had a few pheasants, and I am not aware that any had been lost"*.

The toast given by Major Fitzmaurice at the 'Opening Banquet' serves to confirm Colonel Tottenham's words in that he gave *"the health of the Navvies of the United Kingdom"*, and he spoke of them in glowing terms by referring to their general character and conduct as compared with their counterparts in other countries. Their good conduct certainly appears to be backed up by our research of local newspapers in that no single misdemeanour was considered to be newsworthy in the local press during the whole period of construction of the Llangollen to Corwen line, the only transgression being referred to, and this concerning a navvy on the Ruthin to Corwen line, with the Carnarvon & Denbigh Herald reporting as follows on September 6th 1862:-

DRUNK AND RIOTOUS

George Hemmings, a navvy on the Ruthin Corwen railway was charged with being drunk and riotous at Corwen. Being his first offence and having been in the lock-up since Saturday, he was discharged on paying 6 shillings costs.

The nature of the offence is so insignificant that I feel sure that if navvies were all 'banditti' as well as terrorising the surrounding country as described, newspaper reports by the Victorian press would have detailed such incidents inexhaustibly.

There is no doubting that navvies were often fearless men and took great risks to display their prowess and skill. But what of the numbers that lost their lives in what was undoubtedly the most hazardous of all operations associated with tunnelling with its dangers of rock falls, blasting through millstone, or those men buried by falls of sandstone or tipped out of swaying buckets whilst inside air-shafts with a depth of up to 600 ft - no such records can be established and great doubt must be placed on the existence of such documents, possibly suggesting the utter contempt that railway engineers and contractors had for the well being of the navvy.

Those employed as navvies were usually housed near their place of work since most of the sites could only be reached by foot. Living conditions were primitive and most of the shanties were constructed entirely of mud and turf. As can be imagined, the men were a hard-living and pugnacious breed, but the energy which piece-work pay rates extracted from them was formidable. It is not surprising therefore that disease and death were rife in such conditions. In 1846, the well-known Chartist, Ernest Jones, demanded to know why £70,000 a year was allowed for Prince Albert's horses whilst the working-classes toiled in slavery.

Even the most humane of engineers apparently resigned their navvies to great risk in their work, the most noteable being Isambard Kingdom Brunel. On being told that 131 navvies working on a stretch of the Great Western Railway had been taken to hospital, his comment was that *"this was a small list in view of the amount of powder used and the extent of the heavy work involved"*. Such startling comments place into perspective the regard, or rather lack of it, that the powers that be had for the travail of the navvy. In his book "The Railway Navvies", Terry Coleman states that amongst such casualties were young boys aged no more than five years old.

FIRST ACCIDENT ON THE DENBIGH RUTHIN & CORWEN RAILWAY

News of the first accident on the Ruthin to Corwen section was reported in the Carnarvon and Denbigh Herald on October 12

1861 as follows:

ACCIDENT

An accident occurred on Thursday night to one of the navvies working on the Ffynnogion cutting of the Ruthin to Corwen railway which was nearly attended with fatal consequence. A sudden fall of earth quite covered the man. By the great exertions of his comrades he was extricated from his perilous position, and being promptly attended by Dr Cumpston Jones, the Medical Officer of the line. He is now progressing very favourably.

Black Tom the navvy

The first fatality on the Denbigh Ruthin & Corwen Railway occurred in May 1863 although there appears to be no record of this in any of the local newspapers. It was a report of the second such accident in the 'Baner ac Amserau Cymru' on the 27th May which confirmed this.

The report stated that a fatal accident occurred between 9 and 10 on the morning of Saturday 23rd. A man named Smith (an alias) who was also known as 'Black Tom', was working with a number of other navvies on the 'Trewyn cutting' when some earth fell on him as he was in the act of raising his pick, and that this was driven through his head and he died within seconds. It was thought that 'Black Tom' was Italian and was a man much respected by his fellow navvies. The report concludes in stating that this was the second fatality on the cutting with numerous minor accidents having also occurred.

In the 'Register of Burials 1850 - 1876', burials in the Parish of Corwen (No. 394 in the register), a Thomas Smith, aged 35, was buried on the 25th May 1863, and a Morris Williams (the third navvy to die) in April 1864 (No. 423 in the register).

In the Carnarvon & Denbigh Herald edition of the 30th May 1863, a report of the inquest appears. *"An inquest was held on Monday last on the body of Thomas Smith, a navvy working on the*

DR&C Railway.

Since the completion of the bridge over the Dee the working of the large cutting by Trewyn has been resumed and the soil carried to make the embankment from the bridge to the town. The cutting is of considerable depth, and on Saturday morning last, deceased was loosening the soil.

Contrary to the repeated warnings of Mr Beckingham and his fellow-workmen, deceased would continually keep in advance of the surface, and the surface so hanging over gave way and fell upon him, killing him instantaneously. The head was shattered to pieces, and the body altogether had been mangled in a fearful manner".

The inquest was held at the Feathers Inn before G.J. Williams Esq., Coroner, and a respectable jury, of whom Edward Williams Esq., was foreman. Verdict - "Accidental death". Despite several efforts to locate the place of burial of Black Tom, no marked grave has been discovered.

It is difficult to estimate the number of accidents involving navvies; David Brooke in his book 'The Railway Navvy' states that *"in the twelve months ending 1st September 1840, a total of 40 men were killed on four lines alone. By the 1880's the Navvy Mission Society had been founded and it received information on accidents which in 1883 totalled 289 accidents and 57 fatalities"*, but apparently this was only a fraction of the full total as its secretary of that period was of the opinion that numbers reported were not one-sixth of the actual total.

The 'Baner' does report on one accident with an unusual outcome where one navvy by the name of Jacob Edwards, a native of Llangollen, met with an accident on a cutting near Corwen. His condition was serious and he was 'hospitalized' at the Crown Inn. There doesn't appear to be any follow-up story to establish the extent of the injuries sustained nor the 'treatment' received at the Inn. As the account of this accident was in the edition of 30th September 1865, it must be presumed that this occurred on the Corwen to Llandrillo section, and probably refers to the Llangar cutting.

By the end of 1865 navvies appeared more active in uniting against their employers in matters relating to working conditions, and the 150 employed on the Corwen to Bala railway staged a 'walk-out' in opposing the intentions of their masters to reduce their working hours to nine per day, whilst the workforce demanded to work all of the daylight hours. The reduction in hours would mean a decrease in the navvies's pay by 1s 9d (9p) per week.

Origin of the Navvies

Whilst many navvies came from Ireland, Scotland, Yorkshire and Lancashire, it appears that the Welsh were but a minority in this field, and as we have seen with the fatal accident at Trewyn cutting involving a navvy of Italian nationality, maybe there is much to learn about their ethnicity from their nomadic pattern.

Surprisingly, not many worksongs appear to have survived time - the reason could well be due to their bawdy nature and therefore unprintable, but, as Terry Coleman goes on to say *"...it seems there were few - spectators often remarked on the concentrated silence as a gang of navvies got down to their work..."*. However, in keeping with the folklore of their culture, it appears that where much singing is documented, then the presence of Welsh navvies was evident. There is lack of published material on the nationalities of navvies on the Denbigh, Ruthin, Corwen and Llangollen & Corwen railways respectively, but the Chester-Holyhead line is one such line where many of the navvies were Welshmen who turned out to be a most devout and un-navvy like lot who supported six scripture readers and went to chapel every Sunday, and, as they travelled to their work they always sang fervent hymns in Welsh!

Drawing of Trewyn Cutting in Corwen, scene of two fatal accidents during its construction in 1863 and one the following year.

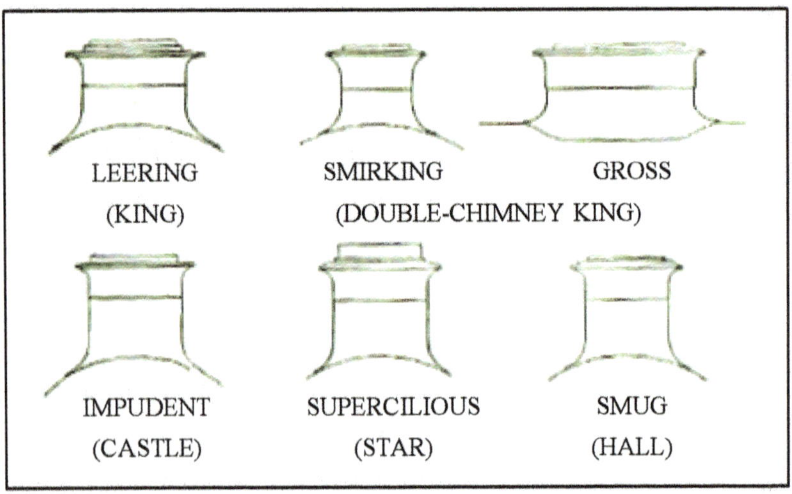

The above illustrations display the copper-capped chimneys which some G.W.R. locomotives had, and each was given its unique impression.

Fitting tribute to an engine driver

The grave in the cemetery of St Mael & St Sulien Church, Corwen, in memory of Owen Owen, train driver who died in 1872, with a fitting Epitaph.

Photo: D. W. Williams

In Affectionate Remembrance of
Owen Owen
Engine Driver
died April 5th 1872
aged 29

His last drive is over, Death has put on the brake,
His Soul has been signalled his long journey to take,
When death sounds its whistle the steam of life falls
And his mortal clay shunted till the last trumpet calls.

Appendix 1

(Ref: Z/CD/60 at Dolgellau Archives and County Records)

Railway Acts of 1859

Llangollen Corwen Railway Company

Sheet No 3 in the Maps, Plans and Sections give the line a total length of 10 miles, 0 furlongs, 6 chains.

(Incorporation of Company. Construction of Railway from Llangollen to Corwen)

Notice is hereby given, that application is intended to be made to Parliament, in the next session, for an Act to incorporate a Company (hereinafter called The Company), with the following, or some of the following, among other powers, that is to say, to construct and maintain a railway, with all proper works, approaches, stations, and other conveniences, commencing by a junction with the Vale of Llangollen Railway, as authorised by "The Vale of Llangollen Railway Act, 1859," at the Llangollen terminus thereof, in or near a certain field, No. 144, in the parish of Llangollen, and county of Denbigh, upon the deposited plans of the said last-mentioned railway, and terminating in a garden occupied by James Maltby, with the Glyndwr Arms Hotel, in the township of Corwen, and parish of Corwen, in the county of Merioneth, and passing through the townships or places of Trevorucha, Llangollen Abbot, Llangollen Fawr, Llangollen Bache, Dinbren, Eglwys Eagle, Rhisgog, Vivod, Pengwern, Maes-yr-Uchan, Llandynon, Cymmo, Coedrwg, Mwstwr, Carrog, Bonwm, Rhagatt, Hendreforfydd, Bodorlas, Trellanerch, Trewyn, Corwen, Ucheldre, Llygadog, Aber-Alwen, Trerddol, Llan or Tirllan and Llansaintfraid, the parishes of Llangollen, Llantisilio and Bryn-

Eglwys, in the county of Denbigh, and the parishes of Llansaintfraid-Glyn-Dyfrdwy and Corwen, in the county of Merioneth; to purchase and take lands, houses, and other property, by compulsion or agreement, for the purposes of the said intended railway and works, and to vary, repeal, or extinguish all existing rights or privileges in any manner connected with such lands, houses, and property, which would in any manner impede or interfere with the construction, maintenance, or use of the said intended railway and works, and to confer other rights and privileges, and to alter, divert, or stop up all turnpike and other roads, railways, tramways, aqueducts, bridges, weirs, canals, streams, and rivers, with which it may be necessary to interfere in the construction of the said intended railway and works; to levy tolls, rates, and charges for and in respect of the use of the said intended railway and works, and to grant exemptions from such tolls, rates, and charges. Duplicate plans and sections of the said intended railway and works, together with book of reference thereto, with a published map showing the general course and direction of the said proposed railway and works, and also a copy of this notice as published in the London Gazette, will be deposited on or before the 30th day of November, instant, with the Clerk of the Peace for the county of Denbigh, at his office, in Ruthin, in the same county, and with the clerk of the Peace for the county of Merioneth, at his office, at Dolgelly, in the same county, and a copy of the said plan, section and book of reference, as relates to each of the parishes in or through which the said intended railway and works are proposed to be made, and a like copy of the said Gazette notice will be deposited on or before the said 30th day of November, instant, with the parish clerk of each such parish at his residence, and in the case of extra-parochial places, then with the parish clerk of some adjoining parish.

And it is also proposed to take powers by the said intended Act, to enable the Company to enter into and carry into effect arrangements and agreements with the Vale of Llangollen Railway Company and the Great Western Railway Company, or either of the said Companies, with the respect to the working and use by the two last named Companies or either of them of the said intended railway and works, and with respect to the interchange of traffic passing over the respective railway of the said Companies, and the apportionment of the tolls and profits arising therefrom, and to enable the said two last-named Companies or either of them, to apply any portion of their income or capital to the purposes of any such arrangement or agreement, and so far as may be necessary for the purposes aforesaid, to alter, amend, extend or enlarge the powers and provisions of "The Vale of Llangollen Railway Act, 1859", and of the several Acts following or some of them, relating to, or directly or indirectly affecting the Great Western Railway Company, that is to say (local and personal), 5th and 6th William IV, cap. 107; 6th William IV, caps. 36, 38, 77, and 79; 1st Victoria, caps. 91 and 92 (1837), and 24 and 26 (1838); 2nd Victoria, cap. 27; 3rd Victoria, cap. 47; 3rd and 4th Victoria, cap. 105; 4th and 5th Victoria, cap. 41; 5 Victoria session 2, cap. 28: 6th Victoria, caps. 10; 7th Victoria, cap. 3; 7th and 8th Victoria, caps. 68 and 99; 8th and 9th Victoria, caps. 40, 42, 53, 115, 155, 156, 184, 188, 190 and 191; 9th Victoria, cap. 14; 9th and 10th Victoria, caps. 166, 181, 236, 239, 240, 250, 251, 274, 275, 278, 307, 308, 313, 315, 326, 335, 337, 338, 369 and 402: 10th and 11th Victoria, caps. 60, 72, 76, 80, 91, 101, 109, 144, 149, 154, 226 and 242; 11th and 12th Victoria, cap. 28, 59, 74, 77, 82, 95, 130, 131, 133, 135, 158 and 159; 12th and 13th Victoria, caps. 6, 7, 55 and 85; 13th and 14th Victoria, caps. 44, 98 and 110; 14th and 15th Victoria, caps. 48, 74, 81 and 131; 15th and 16th Victoria, caps. 117, 125, 133, 140, 145, 146, 147, 165 and 168; 16th and 17th Victoria, caps. 121, 153, 175 and 212; 17th and 18th Victoria, caps. 108, 120, 158, 163, 192, 202, 204, 207, 209, 215 and 222; 18th Victoria, caps. 11, 59, 69, 102 and 139; 18th and 19th Victoria, caps. 151, 171, 172 and 191; 19th and 20th Victoria, caps. 109, 123, 132, 126 and 137, and 22nd and 23rd Victoria, caps. 1, 64 and 120, and of the several Acts relating to the Shrewsbury and Birmingham, and Shrewsbury and Chester Railway Companies, enumerated in the schedule to the said Act, 17th and 18th Victoria, cap. 222. On or before the 23rd day of December next, printed copies of the intended Bill will be deposited in the Private Bill Office of the House of Commons.

Dated the 2nd day of November 1859.

Longueville, Williams, and Jones, Oswestry,

Charles and Watkin Richards, Llangollen,

Solicitors for the Bill.

Theodore Martin,

No 10, New Palace Yard,

Westminster,

Parliamentary Agent.

A total of 363 properties were purchased, 192 in the parish of Llangollen and 171 for the parish of Corwen. Much of the purchased property consisted of woodland, fields, stockyard and buildings and orchards, with a small number of domestic dwellings, stables and coach-houses.

Appendix 2

(Ref: Z/CD/62 at Dolgellau Archives and County Records)

Railway Acts of 1859

Denbigh Ruthin and Corwen Railway Company

Denbigh Ruthin and Corwen Railway

Total length of railway No. 1 & No. 2 - 18 miles, 2 furlongs and 6½ chains.

(Incorporation of Company for Construction of Railways from Denbigh to Ruthin, and from Ruthin to Corwen; powers to use the stations and railways of the Vale of Clwyd and the Chester Holyhead Railway Companies, and for the Vale of Clwyd Railway Company to subscribe to the proposed undertaking, and enter into working arrangements with the Company.)

Notice is hereby given, that application is intended to be made to Parliament, in the ensuing session, for an Act or Acts to incorporate a Company with powers to construct and maintain the following railways, or either of them, with all proper necessary works, stations, and conveniences, connected therewith, or necessary thereto, respectively, that is to say:

No 1. A railway commencing in the town of Denbigh, in the county of Denbigh, by a junction with the Vale of Clwyd Railway at the Denbigh terminus thereof, and terminating in the town of Ruthin, in the county of Denbigh, in field No 1, in the parish of Llanrhydd, in the deposited plans hereinafter mentioned, being the property of Frederick West, Esquire.

No 2. A railway commencing in the town of Ruthin, in the

county of Denbigh, by a junction with the intended railway No 1, hereinbefore described, at the Ruthin terminus of such railway, and terminating in the town of Corwen, in the county of Merionethshire, in field No 1, in the said parish of Corwen, in the deposited plans hereinafter mentioned, being the property of Walter Jones Esquire, and which said intended railways and works will be made in, and pass from, in, through, or into the several parishes, townships, townlands, and extra-parochial and other places following, or some of them, that is to say; Henllan, Henllan Issa, Denbigh, Llanrhaiadr, Prion, Segroit Issa, Segroit Ucha, Llan Llech and Llwyn, Llewesog, Llanynys, Trefechan, Maesmaencymro, Bachymbyd, Bryncaredig, Speddyd and Rhydonen, Ysgeibion, Ruthin, Llanrhydd, Llanrhydd Issa, Llanfair, Eyarth, Garthgynan, Derwen, Derwen Dyfanedd and Derwen Ysgeifiog, Trerplas, all in the county of Denbigh; Gwyddelwern Allthaiarn, Meiarth, Maesgarnedd, Bonron, Maesgwyn, Corwen Trewyn, Corwen Ucheldref, Llangadog, Aberalwen, Dol Aberalwen, Tre'rddol, all in the county of Merioneth. And it is further proposed by such intended Act or Acts, to take powers for the purchase by the said intended Company, of lands and houses, buildings, tenements, and hereditaments, by compulsion or agreement, for the purposes of the said intended railways or railway and works, or some of them, so intended to be authorised as aforesaid, and to vary, repeal, or extinguish all existing rights and privileges in any manner connected with the lands and houses, buildings, tenements and hereditaments proposed to be purchased or taken, or which would in any manner to impede or interfere with the construction, maintenance, or use of the said railways or railway and works, and to confer other rights and privileges, and also to levy tolls, rates, and duties for the use of the said intended railways or railway and works, and to raise money on the credit of the said railways or railway and works, and of the said tolls, rates and duties for the purposes of the said intended Act.

And it is also proposed by the said intended Act or Acts, to take power to deviate in the construction of the said railways or railway and works connected therewith, to such extent and will be shewn or defined on the plans hereinafter referred to, and to break up, alter, divert, and stop up, either permanently or temporarily, as the case may require, all highways, streets, turnpikes, and other roads, footpaths, railways, tramways, bridges, streams, rivers, watercourses, sewers, pipes and drains, within or adjoining, or near the aforesaid parishes, townships, townlands and extra-parochial, or other places, or any of them, with which it may be necessary to interfere in the construction, or for the purposes of the said intended railways or railway and works, and to grant exemptions from such tolls, rates and charges.

And notice is hereby given, that plans of the said intended railways or railway and works together with books of reference thereto, with a published map shewing the general course and direction of the said proposed railways and works, and also a copy of this notice as published in the London Gazette, will be deposited for public inspection on or before the 30th day of November instant, with the clerk of the Peace for the county of Denbigh, and with the clerk of the Peace for the county of Merioneth, at his office in Dolgelly, in the county of Merioneth, and a copy of so much of the said plans, sections, and books of reference as relates to each of the parishes in or through which the said intended railways and works are proposed to be made, and also a copy of this notice as published in the London Gazette, will be deposited for public inspection, on or before the 30th day of November instant, with the Parish Clerk of each such Parish, at his residence.

And it is also proposed by such intended Act or Acts, to enable the Company thereby to be incorporated, or any other Company lawfully using the intended railways or railway, to run on, pass over, and use with their own engines, carriages and waggons, or with engines, carriages and waggons coming to or from such intended lines or line of railway, the whole or any of the lines of railway, stations, watering places, water and conveniences of the Vale of Clwyd Railway Company and of the Chester Holy-head Railway Companies, or either of them, upon such terms and under such payments and conditions, as shall be mutually agreed on, or to fix and determine the amount of rate, tolls, or charge which shall be paid by the said intended Railway Company, for the use by them of the before mentioned stations, railways, works and conveniences or any of them, and also if deemed expedient, to alter and limit the tolls, rates, and charges now authorised to be levied by the Vale of Clwyd Railway Company, and the Chester Holyhead Railway Company, or either of them, in respect thereof. And it is also proposed by the said intended Act or Acts to enable the said Company, to be thereby incorporated, to enter into arrangements for the construction, maintenance, and joint use with the Vale of Clwyd Railway Company of their present or any new or altered station at Denbigh aforesaid (if necessary) to contribute to the expense of making, constructing, and maintaining any such station and the works connected therewith, and to use the same upon payment of such tolls, rates, and charges, and upon such other terms and conditions as may be agreed upon, or as shall be prescribed or provided by the said intended Act or Acts.

And it is also proposed by such intended Act or Acts to enable the company to be thereby incorporated, and the said Vale of Clwyd Railway Company, and the said Chester Holyhead Railway Company, and the London and North Western Railway Company, or any of them, to enter into arrangements and agreements with respect to the working and use by the said companies, or some or one of them of the said intended railways or railway and the works connected therewith or any part thereof, and the management, regulation, and transmission of the traffic upon or over the said intended railways or railway, and the collection, appropriation, appointment, and distribution of the tolls, rates, dues, intended railways or railway and works, or any part thereof, and with reference to the appointment and employment of officers and servants, and to enable the said last-mentioned companies, or any or either of them, to apply any portion of their capital or income to the purposes, or any of them specified or contemplated by any such arrangements or agreement as aforesaid. And it is also proposed by such intended Act or Acts to empower the Vale of Clwyd Railway Company, the Chester Holyhead Railway Company, and the London and North Western Railway Company, or any or either of them, to take and hold shares in and subscribe towards the capital of the said intended company, to appoint directors of the said company, to lend money to the company, and to guarantee to the company interest, dividends, and annual or other payments, and to guarantee the payment of the principal and interest of the mortgage and bond debt of the company, and to raise further capital for the purposes aforesaid, by the creation of new shares, or stock, in the undertakings with or without any preference or priority in payment of interest or dividend, or other privileges attached thereto, and to borrow further monies on mortgage or otherwise.

And it is also proposed to take power by the said Act (if need be), and in lieu of the powers hereinbefore mentioned, for the Vale of Clwyd Railway Company to construct and maintain the said railway No 1.- with the works and conveniences connected therewith, and for that purpose to confer upon the said company all or such of the powers for the purchase of lands and houses, the varying, repeal, and extinguishment of existing rights and privileges, the levying of tolls, rates, or duties, and other powers hereinbefore mentioned, as shall be requisite to enable the said last mentioned railway, and also powers for the raising of capital by the said last mentioned Company, by the creation of shares or partly by such means of fresh subscriptions.

And notice is hereby further given, that so far as may be necessary for the purposes aforesaid or any of them, it is intended by the said proposed Act, to alter, amend, enlarge, or repeal such of the powers and provisions of the several Acts relating to the Vale of Clwyd Railway Company, the Chester Holyhead Railway Company and the London and North Western Railway Company or any or either of them, as are inconsistent with the purposes of the said intended Act. And notice is hereby given, that on or before the 23rd day of December next, printed copies of the Bill intended to be brought into Parliament in the ensuing session, upon which the said Act is intended to be founded, will be deposited in the Private Bill Office of the House of Commons.

Dated this 8th day of November 1859. (continued)

(continued)

William Lloyd, Ruthin,

Solicitor to the Bill.

Edwards, Frankish and Galland,

No 11 New Palace Yard, London.

Parliamentary Agents.

Dec 14th 1859

From a Railway Carriage

Faster than fairies, faster than witches,
Bridges and houses, hedges and ditches;
And charging along like troops in a battle,
All through the meadows the horses and cattle:
All of the sights of the hill and the plain
Fly as thick as driving rain;
And ever again, in the wink of an eye,
Painted stations whistle by.

Here is a child who clambers and scrambles,
All by himself and gathering brambles;
Here is a tramp who stands and gazes,
And there is the green for stinging the daisies!
Here is a cart run away in the road
Lumping along with man and load;
And here is a mill, and there is a river:
Each a glimpse and gone for ever!

Robert Louis Stevenson

Bibliography:

Allen, Geoffrey Freeman, The Illustrated History of Railways in Britain, Marshall Cavendish Books Limited)

Baugham, P.E., Chester to Holyhead Railway Vol. 1, David & Charles Limited

Baugham, P.E., Regional History of the Railways of Great Britain, Vol XI North and Mid-Wales, David & Charles Limited

Briwnant-Jones, G., Welsh Steam, University of Wales Press

Brooke, David The Railway Navvy, David & Charles Limiterd

Christiansen, R. & Miller R.W., The Cambrian Railways - Volume 1: 1852 - 1888, David & Charles Limited

Clinker C.R. LNWR Chronology 1900-1960

Coleman, T. The Railway Navvies, Hutchinson & Co.

Evans D. G., The History of Wales 1815-1906. University of Wales Press

IBM World Book Millennium 2000 Encyclopaedia, IBM

Jones, John R. & Pritchard, A., The Great Little Steam Railways of Wales, Aston Publications Limited

MacDermot, E.T., History of The Great Western Railway, Ian Allan Ltd.,

Moody D. L. CD 2000 Deluxe 1994-2000 Encyclopaedia Britannica, Inc.

Nock, O.S., Steam Railways of Britain in Colour, Blandford Press Ltd.

Pollins, Harold Britain's Railways: An Industrial History, David & Charles

Popplewell, L.A., A Gazetteer of the Railway Contractors and Engineers of Wales and the Borders 1830-1914, Melledgen Press

Rear, W.G., Railways of North Wales (Corwen to Rhyl), Foxline Publishing

Rear, W.G. & Jones, N. Railways of North Wales (Ruabon to Barmouth), Foxline Publishing

Simmons, J. Railways of Britain, Macmillan London Limited.

Simmons, J. Railways of England and Wales, Macmillan London Limited.

Southern, D.W., Leadbetter, H.J. & Weatherley, S.A, Rails to Bala, Charter Publications.

Williams, G.A., When Was Wales?, Penguin Books

INDEX

Abermaw 64

Aberystwyth & Welsh Coast Railway 68

Acrefair 125

Afonwen 132,133

Alberbury 62

Bala
6,11,12,15,20,21,23,29,40,61,62,63,64,65,66,67,
69,91,92,95,96,115,119,

Bala & Dolgelley Railway 40,68

Bala Junction 124

Bala Lake 97,109,110

Banbury 11

Bangor 10,109,133

Bangor Ferry House 10

Barmouth 54,62,63,64,68,114,119,132,133

Barmouth Junction 133

Beeching 1,4,6

Berwyn Station 77,78,111

Berwyn Tunnel 67,70

Bethel 64,65

Betws Gwerfil Goch 122

Betws-y-Coed 70,105

Birkenhead 92

Birmingham 10,44,69

Black Tom 147

Blue Book (report) 56

Bonwm Halt 131

Brassey, Thomas 142,143

Brassey & Field 60,81

British Railways 2, 4,

British Railways Board 4,5

British Road Services 4,

British Transport Commission 4

Broughton Coal ('Black Diamond') 71

Brunel, Isambard Kingdom 12,118,146

Buckinghamshire Railway 11

Bwlch y Rhisgog 67

Cae'r Drewyn 27,37

Caernarvon 26,70,93,105,133

Cambrian Coast 132

Canada 143

Cardiston 62

Carrog 8,81,105,106,118,122,127,129,131,132

Ceiriog Valley 142

Cerrig-y-Drudion 122

Charing Cross 10

Chester 10,15,20,21,44,70,93,121,122,143

Chester-Holyhead line 149

Chester Station 143

Chirk 44,93,142

Conway 109

Coronation Land Cruise 132

Corwen 2,4,6,10,11,12,15,21,22,23,25,26,29,30,
31,32,33,35,36,37,38,43,44,45,46,47,53,54,57,
58,59,60,61,63,64,65,66,69,70,71,81,82,91,92,
93,95,96,97,98,100,102,105,106,107,108,114,
116,118,119,121,122,124,125,126,129,130,147,
148, 149

Corwen & Bala Railway 69,75,94,149

Corwen, Bala & Barmouth Railway 61,62

Corwen, Bala & Dolgelley Railway 94

Craig-Lelo Quarry 126

Criccieth 133

Croesnewydd (Wrexham) 119

Crogen Hall 71,95,142

Cynwyd 64,69,104,114,122,129,130,131

Crewe 33

Davies, David 17,21,28,142,143

Deeside Loop 127

Dee Clwyd Granite Quarry 126

Dee river 21,30,33,36,79,84,117,127

Dee Side Quarry 106

Denbigh 23,24,26,31,43,44,51,59,114,119,121, 126,132

Denbigh Asylum 41

Denbigh, Corwen & Bala Railway Companies 48

Denbigh, Ruthin & Corwen Railway(DR&C) 1,13,14,16,17,20,21,22,24,26,27,30,33,36,40,41, 44,45,47,48,49,52,53,54,55,57,72,93,115,120, 121,122,125,142,143,144,147,149

Denison, Edmund 68

Derwen 57,61,115

Dolgellau 11,26,37,62,64,68,84,102,104,106, 109,124,125, 132,133,134

Dolgelley & Bala Railway 76

Dwyryd 65

Edeyrnion 20,65

Electric Train Staff 129

Ensdon 62

Ffestiniog 12,15,64,68

Ffrith 11

Ffynnogion cutting 147

Ford 62

Garthmeilio (Llangwm) 20

General Strike(1926) 121

Glanrafon 122

Glyndyfrdwy 8,20,70,79,110,111,118,124,127, 128

Gresford 44,93

Gwyddelwern 24,25,26,27,29,35,36,38,46,115, 117,125,126

G.W.R. 12,38,61,66,68,69,93,95,104,115,117, 118,119,122,125,131,132

Hanwood 64

Harlech 62,64

Hereford 69

Holyhead 81

Hughes, John Ceiriog (Ceiriog) 17,19

Humphreys & Beckingham 24

Ireland 149

Iron Bridge 12,15

Johns, Captain 23

Jones, Ernest 146

Key Token Equipment 118

Kinnerley 62

Lancashire 149

Lancashire & Yorkshire Railway 111

Leamington 69

Lichfield 10

Liverpool 58,70,92,141

Llandderfel 6,64,71,102,110,129,130,142

Llandegla 43

Llandinam 142

Llandrillo 62,64,66,69,92,95,114,122,129,130, 131,142,149

Llandudno 109,133

Llangar 106,149

Llangollen 8,12,15,29,30,61,65,66,70,73,74,76, 78,83,98,109,125,141

Llangollen Corwen Railway 1,6,13,14,22,27,36,38,60,61,65,66,67,70,71,72, 73,74,75,76,83,86,96,98,102,107,142,143,145, 149

Llangollen Slab & Slate Company 77

Llangynog 62

Llanidloes 143

Llanidloes-Newtown line 142

Llanrhaiadr 41

Llanymynech 62,63

London 15,44,97,98,100,106

London-Holyhead Irish-Mail Coach 10
London & North Western Railway 1,20,25,38,40,47,56,57,68,114
London Midland & Scottish Railway 1,114,117,119,122
London & North Eastern Railway 1,
London Transport 4,
Ludlow 12

Machynlleth 134
Maerdy 122
Manchester 69,92
Meirionethshire 12
Meirionethshire Postal Directory 115
Melin-y-Wig 57
Milford Haven 64
Ministry of Transport 5
Moel Famau 106
Moel Fferna 124
Mold 11,20,26,43,46
Mold & Denbigh 47
Moody, Dwight L. 53,54
Montgomeryshire 12

Navvy Mission Society 148
Nesscliff 62
Newtown 142,143
Northampton 10
North Wales 3,57
North Wales Narrow-Gauge Railway 105

Oswestry 143
Oswestry & Newtown line 62,63
Oxford 44
Owain Glyndwr Hotel 6,31,71,82,111
Owen Owen 116,151

Paddington 124,125
Padeswood 11
Pant Glas 133
Pale Hall 102
Penarth Quarry 51,98,106
Penllyn 65
Penmaenpool 119
Penrhyn, Lord 57
Pentrefoelas 70
Piercy, Benjamin 23,68,142,143
Piercy, Robert 64,66,142,143
Plack, J.W., 114
Pont-y-Glyn 70
Porth Dinllaen 12,15,64
Porthmadog 62,64,105
Porthywaen 63
Poultenay Smith 72,77,103,114
Pwllheli 133

Railway Mania 43
Railway Passengers' Assurance Company 91
Reid, A. 71,73
Rhaggatt 81
Rhondda Valley 143
Rhug 8,107
Rhyl 31,43,53,54,59,62,121,133,143
Rich, Captain, 72
Robertson, Henry 60,64,70,71,72,73,83,85,86,89, 90,95,102,103,142
Rowston 62
Ruabon 43,44,93,102,104,114,119,124,125,127
Ruabon-Barmouth 3,4
Ruabon-Wrexham 12
Ruthin 20,22,24,26,29,35, 38,46,50,52,59,82,114,132,143

Savin 17,21,38,61,63,68

Scotland 149
Shrawardine 62
Shrewsbury 10,12,15,44,62,64,69,93
Shrewsbury-Chester line 12
Shropshire 62
Slater's Directory 115,125
Snowdon Tourist 4-Horse Coach 92
Southern Railway 1
Stafford 10
Staffordshire 62
St Mael & St Sulien Church 116
Stevenson, Robert Louis 162
Sutton's Directory 118

Tottenham, Colonel 60,70,73,74,78,85
Trawsfynydd 68
Tremadoc 12,15
Trewyn cutting 27,55,147
Turner, Sir Llewelyn 104,105
Tyler, Captain 38

Union Workhouse (Corwen) 40

Vale of Clwyd Railway 19,38,40,51,85
Vale of Edeyrnion 58,127
Vale of Llangollen 79
Vale of Llangollen Railway 12,61,86
Van Lead-Mines 19
Van Railway 19
Vignoles 12,15

Warrington 70,92
Warwick 69
Warwickshire 62
Welsh Coast Railway 61
West Midlands, Shrewsbury & Coast of Wales Railway 62,63,64
Wharncliffe Act 19
Wolverhampton 12,15
Worcester 12
Worcestershire 62

Yorkshire 149

Factfile

Denbigh, Ruthin & Corwen Railway

Royal Assent: *23rd July 1860*
Opened: *22nd September 1864*
Contractors: *David Davies & Thomas Savin*
Engineer: *Benjamin Piercy*

Llangollen & Corwen Railway

Royal Assent: *6th August 1860*
Opened: *21st April 1865*
Contractors: *Thomas Brassey & Field*
Engineers: *Henry Robertson*

Bridges:
Contractor: *Mr Beckingham*

Trewyn
Cutting: *Mr Emery*